COUNT IT ALL JOY!

Count It All Joy!

by Phyllis Thompson

Gospel Recordings

Los Angeles, California

CAPTURING VOICES

Copyright © 1978 by Phyllis Thompson
ISBN 0 340 22447 9

Published in the United States of America as

COUNT IT ALL JOY!
by special arrangement with

HODDER AND STOUGHTON, England

First Printing, 1978

Second Printing, 1980

Third Printing, 1986

or, for the U.S. edition from

Gospel Recordings
122 Glendale Boulevard, Los Angeles, California 90026

ISBN 0-87788-103-0
Library of Congress Catalog Card Number 78-64554

Printed in the United States of America

Contents

Acknowledgments

I AM DEEPLY grateful to many people, especially the members of Gospel Recordings, for their willingness to share the personal experiences and reminiscences which add so much to the interest of such a book as this. To those who, like Mr. David Chapman, Mr. John Gray, Mr. J. Stuart Mill and Dr. Robert Thompson, also supplied valuable background information my thanks are due, also to such people as Miss Doris Gibson and Miss Ann Sherwood who spent hours in going over old records, checking dates and facts and making suggestions. In this connection Miss Marjorie Johnson, Joy Ridderhof's secretary, did a mammoth job with an unwearied patience which won my lasting admiration. The books written by Mrs. Sanna Barlow Rossi provided invaluable material, especially MOUNTAINS SINGING.

The often tedious task of writing was considerably brightened by Miss Ruth Dix whose home provided a quiet haven free from interruptions (except for meals!) and I am indebted to Miss Mollie Robertson for her scrupulous work in typing the MS. Above all I am grateful to Joy Ridderhof herself, not only for all she shared with me, but also for the inspiration of her life with its challenging spiritual secret.

PHYLLIS THOMPSON
London 1977

Prologue

THE CAPTURED VOICES lay silent in the shelves that reached from floor to ceiling in the room behind Mable's office. On discs or tapes, in suitable wrappers, neatly stacked in alphabetical order, there was nothing about them to attract attention. They looked just like recordings stacked on shelves in any other little warehouse in any other downtown area in any other of the cities of the world.

I turned away with a polite smile, and walked back with Mable into her quietly attractive office with its desks and files and atmosphere of ordered activity. I felt vaguely disappointed, as though I had failed to find something I was looking for. I was uninspired.

Then Mable spoke. Her face was suffused with a sudden glow of enthusiasm, and in one sentence she transformed my outlook. The modest office building at one of the innumerable intersections in Los Angeles, with the factory a couple of hundred yards along the road, these unpretentious headquarters of Gospel Recordings Inc., were charged with a significance I had somehow missed. The men and women working in the offices and the packing department, the studios and the pressing rooms, were involved in a campaign of worldwide urgency. It was like finding oneself at the hub of a vast Intelligence Service, with tentacles stretching to the ends of the earth.

What she said was simple enough, though it made a big claim.

'There are more languages here than anywhere else on earth.'

I knew what she meant. On those neatly stacked discs and tapes the Gospel of Jesus Christ had been recorded in over 4,000 languages. In voices that were familiar, speaking words they could understand, the members of over 4,000 ethnic groups could hear the message of eternal salvation. Their voices had been captured not only in towns and cities, but in mountains and deserts, forests and jungles, tropical islands and eternal snows. Quietly and courageously inroads had been made to reach to all the families of the earth, those of every nation and kindred, tribe and tongue.

It was unique. There was nothing else quite like it in the world, and it was still going on. Gospel Recordings wouldn't be satisfied until it had reached the last little tribes, the remotest family groups in the world with the message of God's love spoken in a voice they could understand. And at the source of this unobtrusive though vigorous campaign was a woman with a beaming smile and a spiritual secret with animating power. I knew now what I must do. I walked back across the traffic intersection, up the road to the little compound where some of the Gospel Recordings workers lived, and found her in the communal kitchen, looking in the refrigerator for something to eat.

'Joy,' I said, 'I want to write your story. May I . . . ?'

PHYLLIS THOMPSON

1

Worry is Sin

JOY NEVER KNEW what she had been thinking about on the day she found herself standing half clothed in her room, uncertain whether she was getting up or going to bed. It is possible she hadn't been thinking at all, that being absent-minded merely meant her mind was nowhere, doing nothing. At all events, it was back with her now, and she was faced with the necessity of making a decision. Was it the beginning of the day or the end of it? She could not remember, but feeling sleepy decided it was time to go to bed and acted accordingly. She was comfortably settled and her eyes closed when her eldest sister burst into the room demanding to know why Joy hadn't come to breakfast, and whether she realised she'd be late for school.

'I couldn't remember whether I was getting dressed or getting undressed,' she explained lamely, scrambling into her clothes. When the incident was related downstairs it provided the Ridderhof family with something else to laugh about, and eventually Joy laughed with them. With three sisters and two brothers all older than she to tease her, she had few illusions about herself. She was an absent-minded scatter-brain, like they said.

Gullible, too. It never seemed to occur to her to suspect anyone of mischief. The ejaculation, 'Look Joy! What's that behind you?' would inevitably result in her turning her head to give her brother the opportunity to snatch the banana from her plate with a grin and start eating it. The ruse always worked.

'It's a shame!' protested her cousin, the tender-hearted

Marie, who came frequently from her home in the country to stay with the exuberant household living on the outskirts of Los Angeles' business district. But no-one else seemed to object, not even Mrs. Ridderhof, usually too busy serving to take her place at the end of the table. She might have been expected to reprimand the impudent deceiver, but she didn't. Perhaps she realised that if her youngest daughter were taken in so easily it would be a good thing if she learned early in life not to accept everybody at face value, or to believe everything she was told.

Anyhow, Mrs. Ridderhof had other things to think about, for on her devolved the responsibility of making the somewhat erratic income provided by her husband's musical instruction meet the increasing needs of their family. She managed well, and somehow there was always enough food to provide meals for any strangers who turned up at church on Sunday morning, and to send money to missionaries as well. The Professor himself was satisfied to leave these practical matters in her hands, since they were not at all to his liking. He preferred composing music, for music was his life, affording him the most exquisite joy when well played, and the most excruciating pain when wrong notes were struck. There were times when he rushed out of the house to escape the sound of his own children practising on the piano. He could not bear it!

The Ridderhofs had no money to spare for bus fares, so became staunch supporters of a local evangelical church, trooping along there Sunday after Sunday in their best clothes, a typical American family. From her earliest childhood Joy was accustomed to the procedure of hearty singing and Bible reading, extempore prayer and earnest preaching. The subjects of sin and salvation were clearly proclaimed, and at the age of thirteen Joy responded to the appeal of a woman evangelist to come forward and kneel at the front as evidence of receiving Jesus Christ as Lord and Saviour.

Her mother was somewhat surprised. 'I thought you'd done that already,' she said.

'I was never sure about it before, but now I am,' was Joy's reply, and with characteristic enthusiasm she entered into all the church activities open to her, especially Christian Endeavour, with its emphasis on personal evangelism and leading others to faith in Christ. This was of primary importance to her, and she set about it with a forthrightness that may have displeased some, but which certainly had its effect on others. One of the teachers in the school she attended became a believer through the convincing evidence she gave of what faith in Christ meant. And it was this zeal in speaking of Him to others that impressed the Sherwood family on the occasion when Ann first brought her home to introduce her to them all.

Ann was the youngest of a family in which girls predominated, and they were all teachers. It did not occur to Ann to be anything else, and that is how she met Joy, for they were both taking teacher training in the University of Los Angeles. The two girls struck up a friendship after Joy had invited Ann to go with her to a weekly Bible Club, and when Joy walked into the Sherwood home, bubbling over with delight because she had just visited a Jewish friend in hospital and led her to faith in Christ, she won the affection of them' all. 'We thought it was wonderful that she was already winning souls,' one wrote many years later. 'Her devotion impressed us as far beyond what the rest of us were doing. She was single-hearted for the Lord, as well as being a very attractive-looking young person.'

Apart from that spiritual enthusiasm of hers, however, there was little to distinguish her from other girls of her own age and Christian background. She had no outstanding gifts or acquired skills, and although with her fresh complexion, gray eyes and ready smile her appearance was pleasing enough, her cheeks were too plump for beauty. She earned her pocket money by baby-sitting, she sang in a quartette at church functions with three other girls, including Ann, and had fun in practising, although there was not much time for it. On occasion they stopped their car under a street light for one last practice before going into the church. Picnics and church outings ending up with singing round a camp fire up on the hills added enjoyment to life, and a boy friend, suitably good-looking and suitably earnest about discipleship completed the picture of what appeared a happy and satisfying life for the high-spirited girl in her late teens.

The fact is, however, that underneath her natural buoyancy Joy was neither happy nor satisfied. If impatience and resentment were rarely displayed outwardly, they made their presence felt inwardly, and worried her. There was something else, too. It was fear. No-one who knew her would have believed it if she had told them that the thought of suicide ever so much as crossed her mind. Yet there was at least one occasion when, in her bedroom almost paralysed with apprehension of what lay before her, she found herself exclaiming, 'Oh, I wish it wasn't wrong to commit suicide!'

The particular ordeal that brought about this frame of mind was always the same. She was booked to give a talk in public, either at church or at college, and a nameless, unreasonable fear gripped her. She must stand alone, the eyes of all expectantly fixed on her, and deliver a speech complete with introduction and conclusion and the main points brought out in an orderly fashion in between, and the prospect appalled her. The fact that she usually came through without breaking down or saying anything outrageous failed to give her confidence, and next time it was just as bad.

Preparing for examinations was almost equally alarming. She worried about them for weeks beforehand. 'I suppose worrying goes with being conscientious,' she said to herself reassuringly. It was really quite a good quality. It was not so easy to find a justification for being irritable, however, especially with one's own mother, and for some reason Joy could not explain, there were times when her mother exasperated her. This was all wrong for a Christian, but try as she would the irritation continually cropped up in impatient actions or explosive remarks. It made her feel guilty and ashamed, and the only comfort she could find in that was that at least it proved she was neither indifferent nor hardened, a careless unrepentant backslider. Altogether, an underlying sense of anxiety was perhaps an indispensable adjunct to the Christian life. It might even be an evidence of sincerity, of an earnest desire to become the sort of person God expected one to be.

It came as a shock therefore when the eminent preacher invited for a Victorious Life Conference at the church Joy attended asserted uncompromisingly,

'Worry is sin!'

Joy had never heard such a definition of her permanent condition of mind before. More than anything else Dr. R. C. McQuilkin said in that opening address the simple pronouncement arrested her. That worry was sin, an offence against God as heinous as any crime man can commit, was an entirely new thought. She had lived with worry so long that she had come to regard it vaguely as a sort of uncomfortable virtue. To throw it out, to be rid of it for ever was a prospect at once alluring and alarming. The question was not only whether it was possible, but whether it was right. Joy went home after that first meeting with her mind absorbed by what she had heard. The speaker's strong, melodious voice, the conviction with which he spoke, his reasoned arguments based on the Scriptures had all combined to grip her attention, but it was the promise of deliverance from worry that stirred her most deeply. Could it be true? If you trust you don't worry, if you worry you don't trust sounded logical, but was it possible to be scrupulous in doing your duty without being anxious about it?

The conflict in her mind was intensified by the fact that the series of meetings had been arranged for the very week in which she was to write her final exams. Her normal procedure would have been to spend every spare moment on revision to prepare for any unexpected question she might be called upon to answer next day. Her future career depended on her success in those finals! But instead, evening after evening, drawn by the moving eloquence of the man whose subject was the majesty, the omnipotence, the wisdom of the eternal God, she went to the meetings, although doing so meant studying into the early morning hours to make up for lost time. At one stage, thinking suddenly of the uncertainty of the future, where she would teach if she graduated, and what would happen if she didn't and whether, in the light of everything, it was right to spend time going to the meetings, she found herself exclaiming, 'Oh, I'm in such a dilemma!' and then, to her own amazement, 'And I can't even worry about it!'

That week was the most significant of her life, and had a profound and lasting effect on her theology. The responsibility of man had always loomed large with her, and her Christian life had been lived mainly in dependence on her own efforts, but now the sovereignty of God loomed even larger. The power and the reliability of the Heavenly Father who loved her were what she was called upon to trust in. To doubt Him was unbelief, and unbelief was sin.

She would sin no more. Faith in God should be her attitude, and praise to Him for His willingness and ability to bring good out of everything —.including her own silly mistakes. The sense of freedom this brought was inexpressible, and with it came an overmastering desire to learn more about God who had suddenly become so relevant to everyday life. When she heard that Dr. McQuilkin was hoping to open a Bible School in his home state of South Carolina she went to tell him of her desire, and how much she wanted to enrol and study under him, though there were obstacles in the way. She did not enlarge on them, but made it evident they existed.

His quiet response was simply, 'The Lord will guide you.'

Just that one sentence. That was all.

She had never before heard of God guiding people in practical matters, although she was not unaccustomed to asking His help along the path she had chosen. The thought opened up a new vista of spiritual possibility. If it were true that God actually guided people, that He had a plan for each life, then she wanted to ensure that she fitted into that plan. 'Lord, guide me into the way You want me to go,' she prayed, and wondered if it would include attending the Columbia Bible School in South Carolina for its very first session, or whether it would mean continuing along the way she had already taken, and proceeding with a teaching career.

The greatest obstacle to going to South Carolina was the simple fact that it was some three thousand miles away and she had no money to pay the fare. She might scrape together sufficient to buy the extra items of clothing she would need, she was prepared to risk being without a job when the two years were over, and she could even face up to saying goodbye to Francis for two years, perhaps for ever. If she went to the Bible School she knew she must be free to do whatever it was God might want of her afterwards, and that it would be wiser not to continue a relationship which might normally be expected to lead to marriage. She was ready for all this, but she saw no way at all of raising the considerable sum of money required to get her to her desired destination, and it was evident that if God wanted her there the first step to confirm it would be to have her fare paid for her.

Then one day she received a letter from her eldest sister, married now and living in Minneapolis. Susan, whose second child was only a few months old wrote, 'Would you be willing to come and help me for a few weeks if we pay your fare here and back?' It did not take Joy long to decide that this was the guidance she was looking for. Minneapolis was more than half way to South Carolina, so Susan could pay her fare on to Columbia instead of back to Los Angeles, which would amount to much the same thing. The timing of events was evidently ideal, for she could get to Columbia in good time to be present at the opening of the Bible School. She wrote to Dr. McQuilkin asking him to enrol her, packed her bags, said her goodbyes, and set off. It was the first step towards Africa, towards Ethiopia, where she was sure she was eventually to go as a missionary.

Before she left she heard the result of the final exams on which she had thought so much depended. She had passed with top grades. But somehow it didn't seem to matter now.

*   *   *

It was quite typical of Joy that the thought of paying fees had not seriously occurred to her. She had attended state schools in Los Angeles, and it had always been easy to earn pocket money by baby-sitting. Some of the pleasantest hours of her young life had been spent in the home of Dr. White, looking

after his children and confiding her inmost hopes and aspira-
tions to his kindly, sympathetic wife. If necessary one could
get a job as a waitress in a café, or a cashier in a store,
working at times to suit one's own convenience, and she
assumed it was the same everywhere. Plenty of students had to
work their way through college, and she was quite prepared to
do the same. She had not reckoned on the social barriers of the
south, which in those days of the 1920s were very clearly
defined. The elegant southerners with their soft slow drawl and
their courteous manners, their impeccable family trees and
their negro servants were aristocrats in the eyes of the girl
from cosmopolitan Los Angeles with its booming film
industry, where money not manners determined one's status.
She was very soon aware that her clothes weren't right, that
her shoes were too thick and clumsy, that her speech had a
Yankee twang, and that her ancestry was better not talked
about. She wondered what people would think if they knew she
had a Dutch father and that her Swedish mother could not
even write English, took in boarders, and did her own housework. It was evident that they would be horrified at any
suggestion that a college girl should go out to work. To work!
No woman ever went out to work in South Carolina, except of
course the 'poor whites' who came from their hovels in the hills
to work in the cotton mills, a people apart.

There was nothing she could do to earn money. She would
have to depend on God to supply her material needs, for she
had no way of supporting herself. The monthly college fee of
$25 for food her parents undertook to pay, but where the
money would come from for clothes and books, stamps and
stationery, tooth-brushes, soap, and collections in church on
Sunday, she did not know.

When the money came, mainly in little gifts slipped into
the pigeon hole for letters bearing her name, as far as she was
concerned they came straight from the hand of God. Even
when she knew the donor there was the realisation that God
had prompted the kind thought, and those that came anony-
mously, sometimes with a little card and a text written on
them, were even more precious. She never got over the

wonder of it — that the great, almighty God, Creator of the universe, should notice that she was running out of cash, and send some to her unobtrusively and secretly, just what she needed. The exquisite intimacy of it made her hold her breath and instinctively tread lightly, as though she were in the Holy of Holies. On her knees beside her bed, tears of joy in her eyes, she breathed out her wonder and her gratitude. There were times when the gift seemed too sacred to keep for herself. Like David with the water from the well of Bethlehem, she poured it out before the Lord, doing so in the best way she could think of, which was to pass it on to the Bible College.

For the first year she was there she lived in the McQuilkin home, and seeing his family life at such close range intensified her desire to know God as this man knew Him. She saw him pacing slowly backwards and forwards on the night when his little son was dying, saying firmly, 'God makes no mistakes,' and she knew he meant it. She knew, too, how dear that little boy was to the father who had already lost his first son, and the triumph of trust she saw in those hours was something she never forgot. The Bible College was in its infancy, having started with only four other students beside herself, and the McQuilkins were receiving practically no income from it. It was a period that tested their confidence in God's power and love, and also in His calling, but through it all she never saw anything but quiet assurance, even joy. She knew he was in great demand as a speaker and could obtain high fees for his services, yet here he was, patiently and painstakingly teaching a handful of students. This was the theology that worked, this spirit of thankfulness to an all-wise, all-loving God who works all things for good to those who trust Him, even the things that man and devil mean for evil. The impression made on her lasted a lifetime. The spirit of rejoicing that was to become her distinguishing characteristic was born there.

Her second year at the Columbia Bible College was spent in a different setting. As part of her practical training she lived in a cotton mill village, in charge of the mid-week congregation of workers there. 'Poor white trash' was how some referred to

them. It was her first close association with poverty and
coarseness, for there was much spitting and snuff-taking
among them, and what seemed an inherent lethargy which
prevented them from improving their living conditions. Yet
they came to church on Sunday looking clean and tidy, and
the eagerness on their faces as she told them Bible stories drew
the best from her. 'God enabled me to make them interesting,'
she explained simply when referring to her success along this
line, and as the relevance of what she was relating became
evident the nods and grins or shamefaced sober expressions
told her that she was making her point. The congregation
increased, and the Board Members of the Bible College took
note that Miss Ridderhof seemed to have a special love for
illiterate people, and preaching techniques which reached their
hearts.

When her two years training were completed she was
invited by a church in Miami, Florida, to join their staff and
work among poor people in outlying areas. For the first time in
her life she was in receipt of a regular salary. In addition, she
was provided with a car, comfortable living quarters which she
shared with another girl, and a work which brought her in
touch with people who responded warmly to her friendship
and her ministry. There were members of the church who
became her close friends, and since she saw that God was
blessing the little congregation that was her special charge her
life would have been extremely happy and satisfying but for
one person who, like a wrong ingredient in cooking, spoiled
the flavour. This was the minister's wife, a forceful young
woman with a strong personality who took upon herself the
organising of her husband's newly appointed staff member.
Joy, who knew she was responsible to the minister, found it
was his wife to whom she must give account, and a very
thorough account she was expected to render. Where had she
been on Monday, Tuesday, Wednesday, and every other day
of the week? How many homes had she visited? Where had
she gone for lunch, why had she stopped off at the home of this
or that church member? Had she been invited out to dinner,
and if so, with whom ... ? Not an hour of the day, it seemed,

must be unaccounted for, and reasons must be given for anything out of the ordinary.

For Joy, never renowned for keeping accurate records, this type of surveillance unnerved her. There were times when she sat in her car by the side of the road, trying to prepare her report with tears welling up in her eyes. The principle of trust in God at all times, and confidence in His almighty power to bring good out of evil was deeply engrained in her mind after the years at Bible College, and she tried to rejoice and convince herself that there must be a purpose in this oppression. It did not occur to her to express her dissatisfaction outwardly. Hers was not a reflective nature. A different type of person, equally dedicated, might have reasoned that this was a situation in which moral courage rather than meek submission was called for, that she ought to stand her ground and point out that she had been appointed as assistant to the minister, not to his wife. Joy did not even consider taking such a course. She must endure — and give thanks!

It was an intricate position, and further complicated by the fact that the minister's wife was the self-possessed, efficient type of woman of whom Joy instinctively stood in awe. In the presence of such a one she became conscious of her own haphazard way of doing things, her absent-mindedness, her inability to organise. And when self-possessed efficiency inhabited a tall and well-built person, immaculately groomed, Joy, being slightly below average height, and clothed with only average taste felt at such a disadvantage that her spirit failed, and she acquiesced in anything that did not go against her conscience.

Her flat-mate was in a similar position, for the minister's wife, with probably the best of intentions, started taking a hand in her personal affairs. Her difficulties along that line, however, ended when she married and moved away, leaving Joy in the flat alone, with no outlet for her feelings, and finding it increasingly difficult to praise God from the heart. She was being pressed into a mould entirely unsuitable to her disposition, and the stifling of her feelings brought about the inevitable result. What did not come out went in. The sense of being oppressed turned to rancour against the oppressor, rancour turned to resentment, resentment to secret animosity. So far from loving the minister's wife, she heartily disliked her, although she did not show it. In fact, not being given to introspection, she did not even realise it herself until one day, listening to a preacher who skilfully revealed the subtle iniquities of the human heart, the word 'hate' fastened itself on her conscience.

Hate! Could it be that this was the honest way to describe her feelings towards the woman who was imprisoning her life? She was horrified. She was guilty of the sin which the Word of God asserted was as bad as murder! Once she saw it in that light she did not hesitate to confess it to God with shame and contrition, asking Him to forgive her, and change her attitude.

Then she felt she must go further. She had confessed her secret sins to God, but was not sure that in this case it was sufficient. She decided she ought to confess them to the person involved, the one against whom that poisonous viper of hatred had been inwardly directed. So she went to the minister's wife and apologised for the inner resentment she had harboured, even admitting that she had hated her, for which she asked forgiveness.

Whatever the minister's wife may have felt at this surprising disclosure, she kept it to herself. It probably came as a shock to her to learn that the sunny-tempered girl whose face broadened readily into a smile, and who had apparently yielded so obligingly to her demands had in fact disliked her so intensely that she now felt it necessary to come and apologise. It is not pleasant to realise that one has been hated. Her immediate reaction, however, was quite negative, for she displayed no surprise and passed it off apparently casually. She gave no indication that she was aware of what it had cost Joy to come with her confession, nor did she reveal that it cost her anything to hear it. If Joy had hoped that her apology would be accepted and might even call forth an admission that there were faults on both sides, she was disappointed. Things went on much as before except that Joy, chastened and repentant at the consciousness of her own failure, could accept the restrictions placed upon her without bitterness, and praise the Lord with sincerity. Now she could really believe that He would bring good out of evil. He had restored peace to her heart, just as she had seen Him change the lives and dispositions of some of the people in the little congregation committed to her charge, so she knew He could change the circumstances that still oppressed though no longer rankled.

The change came about in a way that she could not have foreseen, nor would have chosen, for quite suddenly she received news from Los Angeles that her mother had died. When she recovered from the natural sense of shock and loss, she realised that since her three sisters were all married, her father would be alone. The way of duty seemed clear. She must return to do what she could for him, and even her best friends in Miami agreed. As the only single daughter it was obviously for her to go and keep house for him. It meant the end of her period in Miami and the awkward situation which had developed. It also confirmed her feeling that God's time had come for her to move, since a pastor had been appointed to whom her work could be passed on. Now the family bereavement and need had taken the matter out of her hands, and thankfully she prepared to leave, praising God that He had kept her from taking a step that would have been tantamount to running away.

Before she left the south altogether, however, she went to spend a few days with her former house-mate, now living several hundred miles away, and happily married to the man she had chosen in spite of the minister's wife's expressed disapproval. She and Joy had been companions in the same sort of distressing situation, and this had drawn them together. But now that they were out of it they were uneasy about the sense of estrangement between them and the one who, perhaps quite unconsciously, had made life very difficult for them both. They could not just leave it at that, and longed for a change of attitude which would bring about reconciliation.

They did the only thing they could do, in the circumstances. They prayed, and the answer came in a way that surprised them both.

One day, shortly before Joy was to depart, they had been praying together when a knock came at the door. On answering it, whom should they see standing there but the minister's wife!

Smiling and friendly, she stepped inside at their invitation, sat down and chatted without any frigidity or constraint, showing an appreciative interest in their affairs and plans for the future. She made no effort to impose her views upon them or question the rightness of their decisions. Her manner was so different from what it had been formerly that they could scarcely believe she was the same person. She made no reference to what had gone before, nor did she offer any apology for past mistakes, but the fact that she had come to them at all was evidence of a change of attitude, and probably her way of making amends. For Joy it was an unforgettable experience, an evidence of the power of God to alter people and situations in answer to prayer. It meant, too, that she could go forward without any uncomfortable memory of a permanent barrier between her and another. Harmony had been restored.

Her return to Los Angeles brought her again into the same circle of friends she had known before going away, and although some were married others were still single, like Ann.

And like Francis. She had determinedly put him out of her mind on going to Bible School, feeling she should be free for God to direct her to the missionary work she was sure was awaiting her. But no opportunity had presented itself in Ethiopia, and she was back in the same familiar surroundings she had left four years before, with no clear direction from God to take any other pathway than the one she had taken. It was gratifying to find that Francis was still single, and apparently still interested in her. There had been times in the past when his presence had brought an inexpressible awareness of an affinity between them, and when their friends had observed with a smile that their heads were very close as they sat together around a camp fire on a picnic. It had been whispered with knowing nods that a letter from Francis had been discovered under Joy's pillow, and it was taken for granted that they would pair off together. The break of four years seemed to have done nothing to impair the relationship, and once again the courteous, brown-haired young man started ascending the steps that led from the pavement up to the Ridderhofs' modest, sturdy-looking house to take Joy to a church meeting.

In a very short time after her return he broached the subject of marriage. He wanted to marry her, but he didn't make it plain enough for Joy to understand. She was not sure what he meant – perhaps it would be more accurate to say she wasn't sure that he meant it. He had not been in the habit of proposing, and she had never been proposed to before, and somehow it misfired. Francis went away thinking she had definitely refused him, while Joy was left somewhat bewildered, but with her mind made up that she loved him enough to marry him, and that when he mentioned the matter again she would say 'Yes' quite firmly. If he really meant it he would surely speak again, probably during the weekend up in the mountains.

They were both booked to attend a Christian Endeavour camp in the mountains a short time later, and Joy's prayers for it centred a good deal around Francis and herself. If he really wanted to marry her, if what he had said had been his way of proposing, there would be plenty of opportunities among the trees, along the little paths that wound up the mountain side to broach the subject again. She looked out for him the first evening, expecting him to come alongside as usual, but to her surprise he did not. She saw him at a distance, but he did not look in her direction, and she noticed he was talking to another girl, and strolled off with her after the meeting. Throughout the whole weekend he avoided her, though he was quite evidently showing a great interest in that other girl.

So ended the only real romance in Joy Ridderhof's life. It was a grief and a humiliation at the time but it was short-lived. She had already been without him for four years and the exercise of rejoicing in everything that was already the outstanding feature of her faith soon restored her spirits. God was all powerful, all wise, and could easily have influenced Francis to want to marry her if that had been His will. Therefore He must have some other plan for her life.

Meanwhile another disturbing experience upset her for a while. She had returned to Los Angeles for the purpose of looking after her father, but Professor Ridderhof soon made it plain that that was not his idea at all. He would marry again, and to the amazement of the whole family he announced that Marie, their cousin, who lived in Minneapolis, was to be his wife.

No-one had been more surprised than Marie herself when he proposed to her. The thought of such a thing had never entered her mind. He was her aunt's husband, one whom she had known since she was a child as 'Uncle', one whom she admired and respected. Her first reaction to his suggestion was to exclaim with dismay that she couldn't possibly agree to that. 'No, oh no, Uncle!' was her answer. But the Professor was insistent. There was no moral reason whatever why he should not marry her. They were not blood relations, she was only a niece by marriage, and they knew each other so well, she had stayed in the house so often. He needed her. The Professor proposed again, and this time Marie accepted him.

Had her father married any other woman Joy would not have remained in the home at all, but with Marie whom she had known since childhood, gentle Marie who had always loved her, it was different. Once she got over the shock and the sense of rejection the worst part of the new arrangement was the embarrassment of seeing her cousin, less than ten years older than herself, in the place her mother had occupied. She could not possibly foresee at that time all that it would mean to her, how easily and naturally the unique organisation she was to bring into being was to have its birth and development in the place that had always been home to her. All she knew now was that she was free of the two ties that might have held her – Francis as husband, and a widowed father needing her. She praised God for it, not because she felt happy about it but because God was in control not only of the world and the universe, but of her little life as well. And before long she felt happy again. Praising God always had that effect.

She was really free now, free to become a missionary in Ethiopia. But as there were no openings yet, she would prepare herself as best she knew how for a lifetime of service there by returning to college and studying for a B. Ed. degree. She moved back easily into the old round of church activities, a welcome visitor to the homes she had known before going away.

'She was always an influence for good,' said one who traced the commencement of her spiritual life to the night when Joy gave her a lift home, and sitting in her old 'tin Lizzy' faced the teen-ager with eternal realities. In college, though timid, her way of referring to Christ, to answers to prayer, and the wonderful way God worked things for good, allied to the fact that having very little money and experience in selecting clothes she was not as well dressed as her contemporaries, earned for her at least one antagonist who managed to exclude her from the particular society she would have joined. Secret societies were a feature of college life at that time, and the only one that appealed to Joy was a sorority known to be Christian. Her name was put forward, but in the secret ballot she was black-balled. She did not divulge to what degree this ostracism cut her, but when she learned who had been mainly responsible she made special efforts to be friendly. She felt it was the right way to react, to turn the other cheek.

Not so the loyal teen-ager converted in the 'tin Lizzy'. She attended the same college some years later and accepted the invitation to join the same sorority. Then she heard what had happened earlier, when Joy's name came up, and promptly resigned. She wasn't going to belong to any old sorority that had turned down Joy!

These were the years of the great trade depression, when many people were out of work, money was scarce, and missionary societies were affected along with the rest. Joy's enquiries about prospects for qualified teachers being sent to do missionary work in Ethiopia elicited negative responses. There were not sufficient funds available to do more than sustain existing work. When a friend came to her and said, 'Joy, I know you want to go to Africa, and I want to support you,' she felt encouraged, and applied again. Even with the promise of support, however, no society was prepared to embark on further work in Ethiopia and send her there. That door of service was still fast closed, and it did not occur to her that there might be any other. So when, as graduation day drew near, she received the offer of a very well-paid teaching post, there seemed no reason to refuse it. She would sign the contract for a year, and then perhaps the way would be clearer. She might even save enough money to pay her own way out.

All this she explained to the leader of the Bible study group she attended each Sunday. It was gratifying to be able to report that she had received the offer of a good job. She was very pleased indeed about that job, although she did not say so. What she pointed out was the advantage of its being well paid, so that she could save up to go to Africa, and meanwhile, as the Lord had not opened the door there yet, she was prepared to wait His time.

'So you see, Miss Scott, I think I'll take this job for a year, and then see . . .'

She expected a smiling acquiescence, but instead she met with a look of dismay and the exclamation:

'Oh, Joy, you're not thinking that way are you?' Then followed the words that came like a dart from a dagger, draining the smile from her face and leaving her speechless,

'Why, there will be some people on the mission field who will be gone if you wait another year!'

She went home subdued, even alarmed, that night. 'Some people on the mission field . . . gone . . . if you wait another year.' To her the mission field had always been Africa, only Africa, but a new significance was beginning to attach itself to the phrase. The mission field was not just one place or one class of people. The field was the world. There were people in the world today who needed to hear a voice telling them of Christ – her voice – who would have passed into eternity in a year's time. The sense of urgency was so sudden and so powerful that when she got to her room she fell on her knees by her bed, and scarcely knowing what she was doing prayed, 'Lord, whatever door you open, I'll go there . . .'

She did not really mean exactly what her words said. What she meant was any door in Africa. She had no thought of any other continent, least of all the one in which she lived.

*   *   *

Next Sunday, after the morning service, one of the church members who was on the Friends' Mission Board came to her and said,

'Joy, there's a great need down in Honduras. Would you be willing to go?'

2

Marcala

IF JOY HAD not promised God to go anywhere He opened a door it is unlikely that she would ever have considered going to Honduras. Why, it was Latin America! There were plenty of Latin Americans in California and she was not attracted by them. She certainly had no desire to go and live among them. Furthermore, she had not wanted to belong to a denominational mission even though it was evangelical. The 'faith' missions appealed to her more, with their principle of trusting God to provide the necessary finance and making no public appeals for funds. But she had said 'Whatever door . . .' and hard on the heels of that vow had come the specific invitation from the Friends' Mission, followed up quite unexpectedly by the verse 'The Lord will bless you, and prosper you in everything you do when you arrive in the land the Lord your God is giving you.' (Deut. 28.8.) She picked it out at random from a promise box in a friend's house where she had been invited to lunch, and it spoke directly to her in a way she could not deny. The evidence was clear. Honduras was the land the Lord was directing her to, with the Friends' Mission. The friend who had offered to help support her in Africa was willing to be responsible for half her required income in Honduras, and the remainder of her required support was made up by various organisations of the church she had always attended. Within four months she was embarking on the passenger boat that was to take her to her destination, after saying goodbye to the group of friends,

Ann blinking back tears among them, who had come to see her off.

'After I left that sight of our friends standing on the shore waving their handkerchiefs until distance swallowed them up, I realised that the break was made,' she wrote back to them. 'How can people continue to live their lives apart from the power and salvation of Christ when they know that some day there is to be a parting from pleasures, from friends, from home, from honour, from every human and material thing, and they must go out across the bar – alone ... ?' Then she went on to give vivid descriptions of the voyage, from sitting on deck in the evenings 'to watch the moon play intricate and gorgeous patterns on the dark water with her golden shuttle' to going ashore at a Mexican port and seeing people 'huddled in little makeshift shanties along the road, sleeping on their dirt floors and wallowing in dirt and filth ... The market place seemed to be a rendezvous for children, diseased cats and dogs, smoking women, drinking men, flies, dirt, everything.'

Irene and Arthur Schnasse, young workers like herself, were her travelling companions, with Mrs. Cammack, superintendent of the Friends' Mission working in Honduras, in charge of the party. She was a real sport, reported Joy who shared her cabin, and after trying to hold daily classes in Spanish for her younger companions eventually gave up when she realised how tired they were, and took them on sight-seeing trips ashore whenever possible. It was she who awakened Joy, very early on the morning of the tenth day aboard, to get her first glimpse of Honduras.

'Look, Joy! Honduras!' she called, and Joy jumped out of bed to run to the porthole. The boat was moving slowly into the Bay of Ampala among islands so brilliantly green they looked like an emerald necklace. On one side of the boat the moon flung a metallic-like silver pathway along the waters of the estuary, while on the other side the rising sun cast her prisms of light into the sky 'with such an effect that it looked as if she were pouring out jewels of opal, ruby, diamond and pearl ...' Joy did not lack words to paint the picture in glowing colours, nor did she miss the humour of a breathtaking launch trip between the islands in a rainstorm made hilarious by Arthur's chivalrous efforts to protect three women with a raincoat held out with one hand and a big black umbrella uplifted in the other. Impressions and descriptions came tumbling off her pen as she re-lived the seven-hour journey inland on the springless wooden seat of a road-worn bus, with its compensations of beauty, green hills everywhere, and a gorgeous sunset. 'I think of Carrie Jacobs Bond's poem,' she wrote,

> Dear God, how kind you are to me,
> To give me all earth's beauties free!

On arrival about midnight Tegucigalpa the capital looked very unattractive by contrast. A crowded little city with narrow cobbled streets bounded by gloomy, windowless walls, it had a prison-like aspect. 'I must confess I was a little disappointed. I don't know why, but I had always connected foreign mission work with the open fields.' But disappointment was soon swallowed up in the excitement of welcome. 'We immediately went into church and had a prayer meeting – in Spanish, of course, except for us newcomers. We are the foreigners here, and green ones too, I can assure you ... It is good for us to get the tables turned. They sang a song which tells about the time when those from every nation will be gathered Home, and one line says that even the white people will be there. So take hope!'

The people delighted her. 'Whatever my difficulties may be on the field, I know that one of them will not be the difficulty of loving these people. I love them till it hurts. They have such sweet faces ...' though their customs gave her some trouble, such as the gesture for waving goodbye. 'You turn your hand upside down and manipulate your fingers in a way that makes you feel foolish.' The women's method of greeting she found easier to master. Instead of shaking hands they embraced warmly, with a pat on the shoulder. 'Now that I am getting accustomed to that form of greeting I nearly made the break of greeting one of the men that way. I didn't do it, but I nearly did.'

The indomitable Mrs. Cammack was all for getting her young workers on their feet as soon as possible, and encouraged them to memorise Bible talks and even prayers in Spanish, and deliver them at the appropriate times. 'Worse than walking on stilts,' was how Joy described doing this. She always preferred the informal approach and a little later essayed to give a talk without first memorising it. The experiment was not a success. She made 'three awful breaks' and was so overwhelmed with shame and embarrassment at the realisation of what she had said that, as she explained rather primly in her letter home, 'I have not had the desire ever to bring the subject up, not even to the missionaries.' When mistakes were too bad, the simplest way to deal with them seemed to be to ignore them altogether.

Being of an out-going temperament she started trying to converse in Spanish very early, and although her efforts usually ended in general merriment, in which she joined, she was not deterred. Her readiness to laugh at herself always endeared her to people, and the young American Senorita who played the accordion so enthusiastically in street meetings, and had a smile for everyone, became quite a popular character in the town.

She lived in the capital for a year, and although after a few months Arthur and Irene Schnasse moved to take charge of the mission work in the little city of La Esperanza, some days' journey away, Joy remained on. Mrs. Cammack was glad to have with her the energetic young worker who entered in so heartily to the round of open-air meetings and visits to hospitals, and had an unquenchable expectation of seeing penitents come to the front at the 'altar call' in the chapel evangelistic meetings. Joy was eagerly ready for anything, and, even when she was feeling thoroughly ill with jaundice, accompanied her on journeys to remote villages that started on jolting, overcrowded buses bulging with people and merchandise, and ended on mule-back as the trails led farther and farther away from the few roads intersecting the country, up into the mountains.

One of these expeditions led them through the township of

Marcala. In years past missionaries had lived there, but now
the little group of believers, most of them poor and un-
educated, was left without a leader, a handful of despised
Protestants in the midst of a community riddled with corrupt
Roman Catholicism. Some of them came smilingly to meet the
two *Americanas*, the Senora and the Senorita, so glad to talk
with these respected teachers of their own religion, so happy to
see them come, so sad to see them go.

'Will you come back this way?' they asked wistfully, and as
Joy travelled on with her indefatigable leader she was strangely
reluctant to leave the little town.

Marcala. Marcala. Something about it seemed to be sending
out indefinable, invisible cords that were winding around her
heart, tugging at her memories of those gentle, meek faces,
those dark, eager eyes, drawing her mind back to think of
them, those people of Marcala, and to pray for them. After the
crowded days of special meetings in La Esperanza, where Joy,
feeling thoroughly ill, nevertheless managed to face a full
chapel for a daily Bible study in Spanish – 'God worked a
miracle, I was conscious He was doing that' – they passed
through Marcala on their way back. Again there was the deep
sense of rest at being there, as though she belonged to the
place, as though it had a claim on her. Back in the capital,
which for all its narrow dreary streets and dark-robed
populace, its dilapidated adobe houses and crumbling colour-
washed churches seemed very sophisticated compared with the
townships in the mountains, the memory of Marcala persisted,
and as she prayed the impression deepened.

The upshot of it was that she asked Mrs. Cammack if she
could be sent to work in Marcala. She felt that God was calling
her there.

'Everyone wants to go out, not stay and work in the city,'
sighed Mrs. Cammack. 'And anyhow, it wouldn't be safe for a
young woman to be alone in a place like that. As likely as not
there'll be another revolution before long, and then what will
you do . . . ? You haven't seen a revolution yet, you've no idea
how alarming and dangerous they can be.'

God would protect her, Joy asserted, and Mrs. Cammack

had nothing further to say along that line. She knew quite a lot about God's protection herself. The Marcala congregation was certainly in need of leadership, and there was property waiting to be occupied. It was not like going to a place where a house would have to be obtained, and where there were no believers to help in practical ways. But unless there were a reliable person to go with Joy, someone to do the housework and marketing, someone who knew the customs of the country and would protect the gullible *Americana* from crafty money-makers, Mrs. Cammack said she could not agree to the idea. Joy could not go it alone.

In a way, Joy never had to go it alone. All her life there were to be people who came alongside to do the things she couldn't do, without whom her projects would never have got off the ground. If she had no outstanding intellectual ability or academic qualifications, she possessed a certain quality which was to prove of greater value than either. She inspired others. She made friends and kept them, combining an unaffected, wide-eyed appreciation of their talents and achievements with a shrewd recognition of how those talents could be put to good use. When her greatest need was the right companion for Marcala, Cruzita appeared on the scene.

Not many people would have considered Cruzita fit for the job at all. She was only nineteen, she was illiterate, and she was a 'toughie'. The cowboys could control animals no better than she, nor deal more effectively with recalcitrant human beings, either. Arms akimbo, feet astride, she would stand her ground against anyone, giving as good as she got in the way of confident assertion or spirited repartee. Cruzita was afraid of nothing and no-one — except God. Towards Him her attitude was one of faith mingled with wholesome awe. She was learning to read, and her reading sessions were prefaced with earnest prayer lasting for as long as half an hour, beseeching the Lord for His help and enabling for this difficult and tedious task. There was no doubt about Cruzita's spiritual sincerity, and her lack of education combined with fearlessness could be an asset. She would be on the same social level as the vast majority of the people of Marcala, but more than a match for any who might try to take advantage of herself or of Joy. So with the redoubtable Cruzita to accompany her, Joy set off for Marcala.

The arrival of the American Senorita created quite a stir in the town. Unlike the capital, where embassies and trading centres drew a number of people from other countries, Marcala rarely saw a foreigner. Apart from two or three German shopkeepers Joy was the only one, and when she appeared in the streets on Sunday, complete with accordion and Cruzita with a tambourine, to hold an open air meeting, a crowd soon collected. Even the raucous sound of gramophone music issuing from the bars was stopped as the men came out to look and to listen. The members of the little congregation took fresh courage as their new missionary, constantly rejoicing because nothing, nothing, nothing was impossible to her God, urged them on to do and to dare for Him. Prayer meetings increased in number and fervour, and when she suggested that a few days should be set aside for men and boys to come and get some intensive Bible study and training in evangelism, several of them showed a desire to attend. But it meant leaving their work, and that meant losing money, and as they were very poor they wondered if they could afford it.

'Trust God — remember that the Lord Jesus said if we put God's Kingdom first, and act rightly, all these material things we need will be given us,' Joy assured them. As for the meals they would need while they were studying on her compound, she would supply them. She did not know how, for her monthly salary certainly did not run to it, but she would trust God, too. He had made the widow's cruse of oil and handful of flour last for many days, He had made five loaves and two fishes enough food for five thousand people, so He could feed her and her little company on the compound in Marcala just as easily.

Things began to happen very soon. There was the remarkable healing of Juan, her cook's son, for instance. The boy was sick in body and tormented in soul, and his mother was in despair about him.

'Don't despair — rejoice!' was Joy's attitude. 'We must pray and praise! Rejoice that he is ill – rejoice because it is an opportunity for us all to see what God can do. God can heal his body and save his soul.' So they prayed and they praised, and the demented Juan was healed. His mother could scarcely believe what she saw and heard. Juan, cheerful and sane, was eager to work now, and it seemed the most wonderful thing that could happen when the Schnasses in La Esperanza said they needed a house-boy, and were willing to give Juan a trial. Off he went, to remain a trusted servant for years.

Then there was Don Pedro. Don Pedro was a prosperous shoe-maker, and although his morals were no better than most of his fellow townsmen's he wasn't a drunkard, and he did not run up debts in the gambling houses, and he was not quick with the gun in the usual way even if it was rumoured that he had committed one murder under provocation. He had lived more or less faithfully with his latest mistress for several years, supported her and their children quite creditably, and altogether was regarded with some esteem.

His attitude towards Joy was friendly and respectful, and although he did not come to the chapel himself he could sometimes be seen standing at a distance listening at the open air meetings, and one or two of his children came regularly to the children's meetings. Had she been a man, Joy would have made a point of calling in at his shop to talk to him about Christ, but her awareness of the proprieties prevented her from doing so. There were limits beyond which, as a single woman, she could not go without providing an opportunity for suggestive remarks and evil talk. When Arthur Schnasse came over from La Esperanza on one of his rare visits, however, she seized the opportunity to draw his attention to the man.

'Arthur,' she said. 'I've got a feeling about Don Pedro. I feel he might be ready to be saved. Would you go and have a talk with him?' Arthur went, and that same evening Don Pedro, for the first time, entered the missionary's home to find out if there were any way at all whereby a sinful man could do penance, make sacrifice, in some measure at least expiate his own wrong doing, his wrong being ...

It took Joy and Arthur a long time, and much forceful

argument to prove from the Bible that there was nothing he
could do, try as he would every moment for the rest of his life,
to put things right between him and his Maker, but that,
wonder of wonders, it had all been done for him, nearly two
thousand years ago, when the Son of God had died on a cross
outside the walls of Jerusalem. At last, however, Don Pedro
agreed that there was no reason at all for Jesus to die unless it
were as a sacrifice, that such a holy sacrifice alone could atone
for the sins of the world, including those of Don Pedro. Yes, he
saw that. Yes, he wanted to confess his sins to God, and ask
His forgiveness. Yes, he realised God was here, in this room,
the Almighty One who could never be confined to the confes-
sional box. Yes, he would kneel now, come to Him.

They knelt together in the plain little room, the three of
them. Joy and Arthur prayed aloud, as was their custom,
uninhibited, praising God for His Spirit's work in the heart
of this man, praying that he might be truly born of that
same Spirit. They waited for Don Pedro to pray, but he
was silent.

'Don Pedro, have you accepted the Lord?' they asked, and
when Don Pedro lifted his head his face was aglow.

'Have you accepted the Lord?' It had not seemed like that
at all. It had not occurred to him that he was in a position to
accept or reject. It was quite the other way round. His answer
was one Joy never forgot, as with the expression of one who
has been released suddenly from bondage he said,

'He has accepted me.'

*　　　*　　　*

The conversion of Don Pedro created a deeper stir in Marcala
than had the arrival of the Senorita, for he was a well-known
character, and when he openly associated with the Protestants,
standing with them in the open air meetings as well as going in
to their chapel services, the news got around very quickly.
Even more amazing was it that he was soon known to have
done with immorality. He separated from his mistress, and
although he continued to support her and their children, he

never lived with her again, nor was his name ever associated with any other woman.

Such behaviour was unheard of, and evoked a good deal of comment, since this was a new type of celibacy to the people of Marcala. Their priest, of course, had taken vows of celibacy, but in his case they were understood to have meant he would give no woman the protection of marriage and no child the privilege of bearing his name. Exemption from these responsibilities left him all the freer to take his pleasures where he would, and he did not hesitate to make his demands where he chose. Many a boy or girl was referred to covertly as 'the priest's child', and many a husband had to accept the situation, for the priest held a unique position in the neighbourhood, apparently having all the authority of the Church of Rome behind him.

Not surprisingly, therefore, the changed attitude of Don Pedro which merely provided the people of Marcala with a topic for speculation and conversation, incensed the priest to the point of fury. He had been up against the Senorita from the time she arrived in the town. She had seen his thin, angry face as he passed her in the streets, his black robes flying as he strode along. Her presence was an affront to him, an open challenge to his position as the spiritual power in the whole area, and he warned the people in the strongest terms he knew to avoid her. Now it was known that a man in a fairly prominent position in the town had not only listened to her preaching, but was openly aligning himself with the Protestants, the priest made no secret of his animosity. Her life was in danger, and she knew it. The mayor of the town might make a show of providing protection if she, as an American citizen, claimed it, but it was well known that the priest had a hold on him, and that he would do nothing to prevent trigger-happy, hired ruffians from attacking her on the quiet.

One night that is just what was planned. Joy's movements were closely watched, and it was observed that on certain evenings the daughter of one of the doctors came to visit her, and that Joy always accompanied her home. How easy for two men to lurk in the shadows, pounce on her as she returned alone through the dark, cobbled streets, and make a quick get-away after firing a shot! They stalked her as she walked along with Teolinda, saw her enter the house with her, knowing that within a few minutes she would emerge to make her way back to the mission home. It always happened that way.

But on this particular evening it did not happen that way. For the very first time Joy had been requested to spend the night in the house, since the doctor and his wife were going away, and did not want to leave Teolinda alone with their younger children. Neither she nor they knew anything about the two hired assassins, waiting impatiently in the street, wondering why she did not appear. She was peacefully sleeping inside. To some it might have appeared to be a coincidence – but not to Joy, when she heard about it. 'God knew what was arranged for that night – and He made His arrangements!' The story came out soon enough, for the men could not keep it to themselves. As day began to dawn they went into the bar for a drink, and having drunk themselves careless said angrily, 'There we were, sure we had her, and she didn't come back!' The story got back to Joy, and she was told who the two men were. It came as rather a shock to find herself face to face with one of them in broad daylight a short time later, as she walked along the street! The man looked sheepish, but she gave him a pleasant smile, made a friendly remark, and with a nod passed on. It was the best way she knew, on the spur of the moment, of returning good for evil.

The sequel to the story occurred with such dramatic suddenness that the whole town heard about it. Within a week the two men had had a quarrel, one had killed the other, then fled the country, never to be seen there again.

Joy had escaped unharmed, even unalarmed, and people looked with new respect at the Señorita. The God of the Protestants seemed well able to protect her. There must be something in what she was always talking about.

With Don Pedro, however, it was different. He came in for a bad beating up, and at the hands of the priest himself. All the town knew about that, too, and in the end it did the priest's cause more harm than good.

It happened during an open air meeting, when Joy was playing her accordion, a small group of her supporters with her, and Don Pedro, standing slightly to one side, was preparing to preach as soon as the singing ceased. Several onlookers were glancing idly in their direction, among them one of the German storekeepers whose attention was suddenly attracted to someone much nearer at hand. Standing in the shadows of his store was the dark figure of the priest, and in his hand was a revolver. It was trained straight on Don Pedro.

There were plenty of revolvers in Marcala, and a single shot followed by a quick getaway was no uncommon occurrence. If you chanced to be in the vicinity where it was about to happen you had to make up your mind quickly. Either you disappeared, to be as far as possible from the crime so that you wouldn't be implicated, or else you took the law into your own hands and tackled the assailant. The public-spirited German storekeeper, who owed no allegiance to the priest on the one hand or the Protestants on the other, instinctively took the latter course. He closed on the priest, and knocking the revolver out of his hand knocked him over into the bargain.

It all happened in a flash. The priest was down, but his blood was up, and not to be baulked of his prey he leapt to his feet and fairly flew across the narrow street towards Don Pedro.

'You're coming with me!' he shouted. 'You're coming with me to church,' and grasping the surprised man by the nape of the neck started dragging him along towards the ornate but dilapidated cathedral-like edifice that dominated the town.

The onlookers' interest quickened. Maybe there would be a fight in the street! With the priest involved there would be plenty of his adherents to come to his aid, and if the Protestants joined in it would be a show worth seeing. Street fights were common enough occurrences in Marcala, but this would be different, a religious affair with the two sides in open conflict. It might even be that the Senorita would take a hand . . .

However, somewhat to the general disappointment, there was no fight. Don Pedro put up no resistance, but allowed himself to be hauled off while Joy, scarcely aware of what was happening but realising that a skirmish in the street was threatening stuck to the accordion, playing hymns with renewed gusto. Interest between the Senorita on the one hand and the priest on the other was divided, and not surprisingly, the priest dragging away the notable convert proved the greater attraction. Joy was left with a handful of supporters, composed mainly of elderly women, while the crowd followed the priest to the church, eager to see what would happen there. In through the door they surged, to behold the priest trying to force Don Pedro down on his knees before an image of the Virgin Mary.

'Bow down and worship Our Lady!' he demanded fiercely, and for the first time encountered resistance. Don Pedro's head refused to lower itself, and his knees refused to bend. He stood rigid.

'I worship only the true God and His Son Jesus,' he said firmly, his shoulders back and his head held high. The onlookers held their breath. What would the priest do now?

It was at this point that he over-stepped himself. He was so infuriated at his inability to force his will with his bare hands on this obstinate fellow that he looked quickly round for a weapon. His eye alighted on a piece of gleaming metal, his arm shot out, his fingers grasped it, and it came crashing down on Don Pedro's head.

There was a stunned silence, then a murmur ran through the crowd. The weapon the priest held in his hand was a crucifix.

A crucifix! This was sacrilege! Even if you were a priest, invested with mysterious authority from unseen powers, in close communication with the spirits of departed saints (the canonised ones), you didn't use a crucifix, of all things, to hit an unarmed man over the head because he wouldn't do what you told him.

The crucifix was the symbol of martyrdom, of patient suffering, of meek submission to cruelty and injustice. It was something to be venerated, bowed before, worshipped. Even the priest himself performed his genuflexions in front of it. Yet now, here he was waving it about as if it were a common or garden revolver butt, shouting angrily like any other man in a brawl. Why, he'd be brandishing the Blessed Virgin herself next . . . !

The changed atmosphere in the church communicated itself to the priest and he realised he had gone too far. 'Get out! Get out, and never set foot in here again!' he yelled to Don Pedro, then stalked off as rapidly as he could, leaving his victim to stagger away, his hand up to his head, the blood trickling through his fingers.

He knew where to go. Joy and her small band were in the chapel, praying for him.

'Don Pedro, you've had the privilege of suffering for your Lord,' she said, deeply moved, when she saw him. It was not the only time Don Pedro had that privilege. During one of the periodical revolutions which seemed to occur every two years, there was a fracas outside the chapel where special meetings were being held. A crowd of men rushed in brandishing revolvers and knives, and dragged off to jail the visiting evangelists as well as members of the local congregation. Some of them got a beating up before they were released the next morning, and Don Pedro did not escape.

Cruzita escaped, however. She was taken off with the rest of them but was soon let out, arriving back at the mission in the early hours of the morning. She was somewhat disappointed. 'I wish I could have stayed on in jail, to encourage the others,' she told Joy. So far from being intimidated by threats and danger, she seemed to thrive on them. Revolutions usually resulted in the mission compound being crowded with frightened people, girls especially, who crept in to escape the violence and the lust of the riff-raff who took advantage of the prevailing disorder. The American flag seemed to promise protection, but it did not always deter the excited, feverish men who rushed round the streets from besieging the mission home, pounding on the doors and shuttered windows demanding to be let in. Joy had her hands full, trying to soothe hysterical girls and urge the believers to faith and prayer in their extremity.

'To say the least they were tense days. I often thought what would happen if I should give way to fear for one minute. The poor people who had come to seek refuge, and there were many, some nights as many as forty spent the night here, only felt safe when they could be near me, to touch my hand, or beg me to pray for them to my God that nothing would happen. He kept me in peace.' Then she added,

'And my faithful, loyal courageous girl companion Cruz.'

The courage of Cruz reached its peak on the night when a rabble of men were outside, banging on the door and shouting. Suddenly the door opened, and out stepped Cruzita, head high, eyes unafraid and indignant. Shutting the door behind her she stood there, her hands on her hips and in a loud stern voice cried,

'Stop! Stop I say! Stop that noise. Where is your general? I demand to see your general!'

The confident attitude of authority of the well-built girl who stood before them had a remarkable effect on the men. Perhaps they sensed, even though they did not see, that she did not stand there alone. They stopped their shouting and gaped at her, falling back as she moved towards them.

'I demand to see your general!' she said again, and instead of closing in on her they made way. Down the street she marched, to the headquarters of the local general, a man who in times of peace was usually drunk, but in times of revolution managed to remain sober. Cruzita strode up to him, stated the case of the beleaguered American Senorita, and firmly requested him to come and intervene. Within minutes she was on her way back, accompanied by the general, who wrathfully sent the rabble about their business.

Revolutions not only brought danger, they brought privation. Normal trading came to a standstill as people were afraid to venture along the country roads and trails to take their produce to market. With twenty or thirty people sheltering in the mission compound, all needing to be fed, Joy began to experience what it meant to rely on God for daily bread. She had read with admiration and avidity the records of George Müller of Bristol's work of faith among orphans, and marvelled at some of the things that happened in answer to his prayers when there was literally not enough food to provide for one day more. Now she had the opportunity of proving God in the same way — in fact, she may be said to have had no option. If God did not provide, they would all go hungry. The life of faith in Him to send money and means as they were needed for the work He gave her to do struck deep roots in those days of revolution. There were times when she told the people who were with her that there was something to praise God for, something to rejoice about. 'We've got no food left. Rejoice! Rejoice that our wonderful God will hear us when we pray — pray and praise. Somehow He will send us what we need.'

One such occasion had a particularly dramatic note about it, for after they had prayed Joy said, 'Now we must look for the answer. It must be on the way.' She glanced down the road, and then exclaimed, 'Why, that must be it!' Coming down the trail was Juan, healthy and happy and driving a pack-mule. He beamed with delight at the welcome he received as he entered the familiar compound. Arthur and Irene Schnasse, in the midst of turmoil even more harrowing than in Marcala, had nevertheless remembered their lonely colleague and sent a load of stores from La Esperanza which arrived with almost theatrical timing.

Joy passed through two revolutions in Honduras, and in 1934 a third was just beginning when it stopped abruptly, and as far as Joy was concerned that happened because of Don Pedro's prayer. Official warning had been given that the revolution would reach the district around Marcala in a matter of hours. Once more lawlessness and plunder, looting and murder would disrupt normal life. Travel outside the city would be too dangerous and too uncertain to embark on, and the frequent visits made to remote villages for evangelism and teaching would have to cease.

Don Pedro's spirit was stirred. He was not prepared to accept the situation, and in an urgent prayer meeting he told God so.

It was one of the outstanding experiences of Joy's life, listening to Don Pedro talking to God the way he did that evening. He said, in effect, that this state of affairs must not

continue, since revolutions hindered God's work. Preaching
was held up. Visiting was held up.

'Thy people away up in the mountains suffer and we can't
help them. They need encouraging, they need to be taught Thy
Word and we can't get to them. The people here in Marcala
are afraid to come out on the streets, so they don't come to
hear Thy Word. Lord, this is not Thy will, and it's not ours
either. We refuse to accept this situation. Satan is behind it,
and we stand against him.' Then he went on to make it clear
that he was looking to God to put a stop to it. His attitude was
respectful, rather like that of a trusted servant explaining
something to his employer in the assurance that he had gained
a hearing and that his reasonable request would be attended to.
When he concluded what he had to say he seemed quite
confident that the matter was in hand.

The revolution came to an end quite soon after that, and
whatever explanations the politicians or economists had to
give in later years when the country entered a long period of
peace in marked contrast to the repeated upheavals of the past,
the little congregation in Marcala had no doubt of the real
reason. Don Pedro had gone in before God to argue the case
against revolutions in Honduras, God had heard him and
acted according to his request. The opposition of the priest
continued unabated, there were inevitable disappointments in
the work which, as Joy expressed it, 'always has present this
duet – trial and triumph', but there was no more complete
disruption of life. Violence and oppression were local affairs
only, and there were times when the tables were turned on the
culprits as when a noisy gang of trouble makers outside the
chapel were throwing stones one of which hit full in the face
the chief of police, who happened to be passing by at the time.
The Gospel meeting proceeded in peace, while the gang spent
the night sweeping the jail.

The mayor and council, too, did not find things going all
their own way when they summoned Joy to appear before
them and forbade her to hold any more open air meetings. Her
spirited reply was that as long as the Catholics were allowed to
have their processions in the streets she would not give up the

privilege of preaching in the streets. The affair got to the ears of the Government, and to their discomfiture the mayor and council received a severe scolding — 'So now we are freer than ever.'

Joy's letters home during those years were full of reports of what was going on — trips to the mountains, the establishing in Marcala of a two-months' Bible School, visits to conferences in other centres which involved travelling on lorries — 'going we went as cargo and coming back as baggage, to save on fares.' She gave names and thumb nail sketches of people who had come to faith in Christ, and mentioned also her little garden that she was too busy to work in herself, so had divided it up for church members to grow things in. 'I also have several chickens, a little turkey, two small ducks, a cow and a calf. Last but not least I have a cat and a parrot. They were gifts, so what can one do!' When her friends wrote to ask if there was anything she would like them to send her, her fertile mind produced suggestions of forty little items that would be useful for her girls' club, for the Sunday School, for handwork, for helping the poor — old picture cards, second-hand clothing, pins, crayons, cuttings from newspapers that would provide illustrations for sermons ... Offers of help were always accepted and when little parcels came pouring in she assured the donors that everything was useful and everything was welcome. 'Who sent me these lovely dresses and shoes? They got here the day before Christmas — my other shoes were terrible. The dresses are *so* becoming ...' She was far too busy to bother about her own clothes, and scarcely realising how it happened she found that her Heavenly Father had His own ways of looking after that aspect of her life. 'Oh, I feel so unworthy of the least of God's blessings and especially the privilege of being ambassador of the realms above.' Her letters breathed praise to God, more than anything for His evident working in human hearts. 'There is a fervent spirit of prayer and a number arise at 5 o'clock in the morning to pray for revival. The believers are personal workers, and are trying to win their comrades to Jesus Christ.'

She was so buoyed up by what was happening, with

scarcely a week passing when there was not news of one or another having come to faith in Christ, that she paid no attention to her feelings of weariness, of nausea, her lack of appetite. She wrote frequently to 'my dearest Mrs. White', her doctor's wife in Los Angeles, and occasionally asked for some medicine for persistent digestive troubles, because they were a nuisance, but otherwise she just went on from day to day. There were too many people to visit, too many classes to prepare for, too many meetings to speak at, too many gatherings for prayer to leave her time to think about herself. She was getting thinner, her eyes were unnaturally bright, there was a nervous twitch on the left side of her face when she talked, but there was no-one to notice it until a missionary from the north coast came to Marcala on a friendly visit. Joy's appearance alarmed her, and she spoke urgently,

'Joy, you're ill. You need to get away from here and have a complete rest. You ought to see a doctor. If you don't, you'll crack up completely.' She spoke in a solemn voice, and added,

'And you'd better go soon. Something could be developing that would affect your health for the rest of your life. If you want to come back, don't delay.'

'If you want to come back . . .' The words arrested Joy. Of course she wanted to come back! She had no other desire in life but to be in Marcala. Yes, she admitted, she wasn't feeling too good, she was having unpleasant evidences that something might be wrong. She'd been away from home for about six years, so she was due for leave. She'd go as soon as it could be arranged, so that she could get back all the quicker.

She went back to Los Angeles in 1936, and did not see Marcala again for eight years.

3

In the Beginning

MEMORY HAS AN unpredictable way of high-lighting the unimportant. In the months that followed Joy's return to Los Angeles, when she spent more time on her bed than on her feet, plagued with a physical condition which did not respond either to the doctor's medicines or the prescribed rest, the things she remembered about Honduras were not the tensions and the dramas and the spiritual triumphs so much as the simple, everyday happenings, the ordinary people. The grass-roofed stalls in the markets, the lank-haired country people, the sudden fear of the mangy, snarling dogs – 'I was much more frightened of the dogs than of the priest,' she often said – the sound of maize paste being slapped in the hands of women preparing their bread, and the clippity-clop clippity-clop of her little mule carrying her up the mountain paths to remote hamlets and villages. Even there the raucous screeching of worn gramophone records played with blunt needles struck a discordant note. The gramophone, like Singer's sewing machine, had penetrated to the most unexpected places, and sometimes proved as formidable an opponent as jeering on-lookers, with the incessant noise drowning the voice of the speaker.

'I wish there were Gospel records in Spanish,' she had once heard a missionary in Honduras say wistfully while listening to hymn-singing in English on her own gramophone. 'If only they could hear this in their own language, what an impact it would make!' She thought of that remark often while lying in her attic bedroom in the Ridderhof home in Witmer Street. One such record would have proved more effective than the special visit she had made to a poor little widow with several children living about eight miles out of Marcala. She had spent a whole day with her, just before leaving for furlough. It had cost her much physical effort, and had apparently been fruitless. The little widow, her mind weakened by poverty and sorrow and anxiety only got confused when she tried to concentrate, and Joy, returning to Marcala at the end of the day, knew she had not memorised one sentence correctly. When would she again hear a human voice speaking to her the words of God?

The inactivity of those months in Los Angeles gave Joy more time than she desired for solitude and reflection. All her life she had had so many interests, so much to do, that to lie idle day after day tested her faith and cheerfulness in a new way. The habit of rejoicing in everything was well engrained, however, and stood her in good stead when boredom and depression assailed, but there were times when it required a deliberate effort of the will to be maintained. The most insidious encroachment on her confidence in God's sovereignty and love came through the inexplicable nature of her illness. Neither the prayers of her friends nor the advice of her doctor appeared to have any effect. Her hope of returning to Honduras began to fade, for even after a long spell in Columbia, at the Bible College where she enjoyed to the full attending some of the lectures, she still had little energy for anything else, and got back to Los Angeles scarcely any better than when she had left. And the question was being asked covertly,

'What *is* the matter with Joy? Is she just imagining she's ill? is it something in her mind?'

She would have been more – or less – than human if the possibility that her condition was in some measure a matter of the mind left her unaffected. Was she indeed a hypochondriac? No amount of rejoicing seemed to be making any difference, so if God did not heal her, then she'd rejoice in that, too. God must have a purpose in it.

All the same, it was a tremendous relief to her when she eventually met a missionary doctor home from China who assured her that she was no hypochondriac. When she confided in him, telling him her symptoms, he knew immediately what was the cause. He had treated others with the same complaint in China, he told her. Her trouble was caused not only by dysentery and malaria, but by an amoeba very rare in the United States. Doctors in California could not be expected to recognise it. But with his experience he had no doubt but that she was suffering from amoebic hystolytica and that he could give her the necessary treatment.

Joy did not mind in the least what it was she had, so long as it was something medically explicable. She had an amoebia, not a phobia! She could not have been more delighted. There was a physical, not a psychological explanation for her condition, and the knowledge was such a comfort she began to feel better immediately. Although full health returned but slowly she was no longer in the state of uncertainty that had tested her for so many months. And now the purpose of it all began to become clearer. It was during this very time of inactivity that the thought of Gospel gramophone records in Spanish had come to mind again and again, although she had not felt she could do anything about them herself. But a chance meeting with a man with some knowledge of technical matters made her realise that there might be something she could do — although she often said in later years that if she had known all that was involved she would probably never have embarked on the scheme. As it was, the idea was now in her mind, and she could not keep an idea like that to herself. A Gospel gramophone record in Spanish! She talked about it to her friends at home, and wrote about it to her friends in Honduras. 'Let's pray about it,' she urged, and confident that God would do something, she decided she would be prepared as best she could. The records ought to contain some music so it would be useful if she could learn to play the guitar. 'It's something I can do while I'm inactive,' she thought. She was getting into line now, although she did not know it, approaching the highway of God's plan for her life work that had been hidden from her until now, and for which the years in Marcala had been a preparation. Just as the chance meeting with the missionary doctor from China had revealed the basic cause of her mystifying illness, just as another chance meeting had opened her eyes to the possibility of producing records, now the decision to learn to play the guitar led to the final step which was to bring her right on track.

'Why are you learning to play the guitar?' her instructor enquired casually one day.

'I'm hoping to make gramophone records of Gospel messages and songs in Spanish, and I'll need music,' Joy explained. 'I don't know anything about the mechanical side of things, so I'm waiting for the Lord to lead about that.'

The instructor was interested. 'I know a missionary in Pasadena who's back from Central America,' he said, 'And he's installing professional recording equipment in his home. He plans to start up in the business. I'm sure he'd help you. I'll put you in touch with him . . .'

The missionary from Central America was not only able, but willing, to help her. He would produce the records on a non profit making basis for her. The studio he was fixing up was draped with blankets and muffled with quilts, a thoroughly home-made affair, but he was confident the result would be perfectly satisfactory. Arrangements were made, and a time fixed for Miss Ridderhof to come along and make her first recording. The date arranged was the last day of December, 1938.

'I have enough money in hand for four master records (two discs). They are $7.50 each, just half the regular cost. The recording work . . . is about to be launched!' she wrote.

She made her plans. Play some background music of the type the people of Honduras liked, read selected Bible verses interspersed with a few explanatory comments, perhaps a little singing . . . A friend who was an accomplished pianist responded enthusiastically to the invitation to come and play.

'And I'm sure Virginia would drive us out to Pasadena if she's free,' she added. So Virginia Miller took the wheel and drove along the highway to Pasadena on that memorable night, knowing next to nothing of what was to be recorded, having no foreknowledge at all as to how it would all affect the course of her own life. From her point of view she was merely obliging a friend by giving her a lift. She wasn't in the least interested in what went on in the studio.

For Joy, however, it was the culmination of hours of planning and praying during the misty period in which the only hope she had of doing anything for the people of Honduras was to produce a Christian gramophone record in Spanish. Now at last she had done it, and when she heard it played back, observed how accurately the modulation and emotion in her voice had been reproduced, knew that the message of God's love had come over in a way Spanish-speaking people could understand, an inexpressible sense of relief and joy flooded her being. She could not have explained it. She had no conscious revelation that a key was being placed in her hands that would open the door for people in thousands of different languages to hear the news about the Son of God in their mother-tongue. What happened to her when she listened to her first Spanish record can best be likened to the welling up of a hidden spring of oil that has at last been struck, and now gushes out unquenchably. The ecstasy of that fleeting experience was out of all proportion to the immediate cause, the production of one gramophone record. For one mystical moment it was as though a curtain veiling the future was drawn back that she might sense the accumulated joy of many hearts. Whatever it was, it resulted in an unchangeable, deep-seated conviction that this was an appointed task — the production of Gospel records. At that time she had no thought of producing them in any other language than Spanish.

She had no more than two dozen records made of that first programme, and having found out the way they should be packed and mailed, she got them ready and posted them off — some to Don Pedro in Marcala, some to Mrs. Cammack in the capital, some to the Schnasses in La Esperanza, some to members of the Central American Mission in Honduras. Then she started planning the next record, while waiting eagerly for reactions from those who listened to the first one.

The letters she received exceeded her highest hopes in their enthusiasm. She was almost sick with excitement. The record was wonderful! People had listened to it wide-eyed, wanted to hear it again and again, and not only the believers, either. Some who had been utterly indifferent or even strongly opposed were strangely moved by it. Their attitudes were completely changed, they were showing interest as never before. The songs and the verses had been heard so often people knew them by heart, could repeat them just as they had heard them – American accent and all!

'American accent and all!' Joy laughed, but she shook her head. Though her Spanish was fluent enough, she knew she didn't speak it as a native. From now on she would prepare the scripts, but the voices that spoke the words must be those to whom Spanish was their mother tongue. There were plenty of Mexicans and Latin Americans in Los Angeles, and she had little difficulty in finding those who would help to make Gospel records. So she prepared scripts and arranged visits to the studios, and the more records she sent to Honduras the greater was the demand for them.

'They work longer hours than we can!' was the gist of the messages she had from the missionaries. 'We can hear them being played at night as we go off to sleep. They stay around when we have to leave, and we can depend on them always saying the same thing, and not being put off by hecklers! They preach to a crowd of onlookers at a fiesta while we talk to enquirers.' There was a group of Spanish speaking Indians who had become Christians but had no pastor, or anyone to teach them – the records were just what they needed. So the reports came in, and there were times when Joy was so excited that she could not trust herself to open the letters herself. 'You read it to me,' she would say to whoever happened to be with her.

As the months rolled on, Joy's bedroom looked more and more like an office-cum-packing-room, less and less like a bedroom. She wrote letters, compiled programmes, stacked records and packed them for dispatching, and there were times when she stood bewildered, looking for somewhere to put the things that were strewn over her bed because she couldn't get into it while they were there, and there was no more space even on the floor. It was a pity one had to sleep when there was so much to be done, with orders coming from as far away as the Canary Isles. Health was returning unnoticed until it occurred to her that she was feeling as well and working as energetically as when she was in Honduras. Why, she was fit enough to go back now! First she must reach her goal of producing fifty record programmes, then she would make tracks for Marcala again! The hope provided an added incentive to complete the work that remained to be done.

Perhaps that is why, when she received a letter asking if she would produce records in the language of the Navajo Indians, she hesitated. The missionaries who had approached her assured her that they knew a fine Navajo Christian whose voice could be used, and that they would personally accompany him to Los Angeles, to do the translating and tell him exactly what to say. They would meet all financial outlay, if only Miss Ridderhof would undertake to produce the records.

To respond to this request would not entail a great deal of extra work on her part, nor need it unduly delay her return to Honduras. She knew that. The question was, what would it lead to? If she once moved on from Spanish to any other language, where would the thing stop? She already had extended far beyond her original aim of providing something for the people of Honduras, especially those in the area where she had worked. The records were being sent far and wide now, among the 300 million Spanish speaking people of the world. She did not want to extend her activities to the Navajo Indians, because it might lead on to something else, and hinder her return to Honduras.

But she knew she had to do it. 'I have other sheep that are not of this fold; I must bring them also, and they will heed My voice . . .' the Good Shepherd had said, and was He not still saying it? The impulse of His own yearning compassion for those sheep still beyond the sound of His voice seemed to reach her, and even the longing she felt for her own mountain folk was subdued.

'Lord,' she said, 'I'll make recordings in as many languages as you want me to.'

It was the same sort of step she had taken when she had relinquished her determination that Ethiopia was the mission field to which she should go, and had said to the Lord, 'Anywhere ...' So she told the missionaries to the Navajo Indians that she would produce records for them.

Then Ann Sherwood joined her. It all came about in such a natural and unpremeditated way that it would have been difficult to define exactly when Ann became a member of Gospel Recordings. Joy had given up her church work in Miami because of home circumstances, and now Ann gave up her teaching post in Seattle for a similar reason. Her mother was seriously ill, and Ann returned home to nurse her until she died.

The two friends had not met for ten years, but slipped back into the old relationship as though time meant nothing. Joy enthusiastically told of what she was doing, and Ann went to see for herself. After a few visits to the bedroom with the typewriter, the packing cardboard, the piles of records and the accumulating stack of letters waiting to be answered she asked,

'Joy, would it be any help if I came along a couple of afternoons each week to do some letters for you? I can be typing them while you get on with something else.'

Joy never refused an offer of help, and this one was too good to be missed. Her response was immediate.

'Why, Ann, it would be just wonderful!' And when Ann discovered that the desk drawer into which letters were slipped contained all Joy's accounts as well, scribbled on the backs of used envelopes, and eventually showed Joy a little account book into which they had all been neatly entered, Joy beamed her delight, 'Ann, that's just fine!' and looking at the tidy drawer observed, 'That drawer was bound to get filled up sometime.' It was always a relief to find an empty space. Then other things claimed her attention. 'What do you think is the best musical setting for this song? We need something to help fix the words in the mind ...' And since Ann had musical training and experience she invariably helped at rehearsals of the score she had selected, until eventually most of her time was spent on the work. One day Joy mentioned it.

'I don't know how I'd ever manage without you, Ann,' she said. 'You're giving all your time to this project, and I've no capital and no regular income. I'll never be able to give you any money, any sort of a salary . . .'

Ann looked at her and asked simply,

'How do you manage yourself?'

Just as simply Joy told her.

'I just look to the Lord. It's His work I'm doing. I know that. So I trust Him to give me what I need, and He does.'

'Well,' said Ann. 'I can trust Him to do the same for me.' So that matter was settled, once for all. The brief conversation revealed the foundation upon which they were building, and which was to be the foundation for which Joy always looked in later years when people applied for membership in Gospel Recordings. Unless they gave convincing evidence that God had called them into this particular branch of His work, and unless they were prepared to trust Him to supply them with what they needed for the task assigned to them she could not accept them. Faith was the primary requirement. Without it every other quality lost its value.

Back there in the beginning of things, however, in 1941, no thought of receiving members crossed her mind, nor even of forming an organisation at all. She and Ann exclaimed rather delightedly at some of the letters that came addressed to 'Spanish Gospel Recordings', and commenced,

'Dear Sir,
    Can your organisation supply us with 100 Spanish
    records . . .'

Your organisation! They looked around the crowded little attic bedroom and chuckled. The idea of being an organisation had not seriously occurred to them until those letters began to arrive. Eventually they realised that it would clarify things legally if they were duly registered, so Joy took the necessary step. There was nothing much to it, she affirmed. It wasn't nearly so important as getting their own studio and doing their own recording. This was a step she was deciding must be taken, and it was demanding both faith and mental effort. She did not know where the money was coming from to build a studio, and at the age of nearly forty it was not so easy to master the techniques connected with successful recording. Ann was better at it than she was. But it had to be done. The synchronising of the arrival of performers with the booking of commercial studios was proving too difficult. Time and opportunities were being lost as tribespeople were brought to Los Angeles especially for the purpose of recording, only to be met with constant frustration because commercial studios were not always available when needed.

'Rejoice!' said Joy when it happened time and time again. 'Rejoice – the Lord has a purpose for good in it all.' The decision to ask Him to give them a studio proved to be the purpose in this case, and once she had made it the confirming evidence was provided.

The first thing was the building. Where could they find it? The nearer to her attic the better, of course, but even she was surprised to find it lying patiently waiting to be recognised so to speak, in the back garden. She was looking across the familiar stretch of lawn one day, and her glance fell on the battered shed that was partly hidden by an old gnarled tree. It had been there for as long as she could remember. Its days of usefulness as a stable over, it had become the junk shed. Dilapidated and full of rubbish it nevertheless had a good roof, and once cleared out and cleaned up there was no reason why it should not be made into a studio. Joy and Ann with some cheerful volunteers set to work.

During the course of this clearing out and cleaning up process Joy received the first official offer to join the staff of Spanish Gospel Recordings. It was from Virginia Miller, who had continued to take her friend, the recording pianist to studios when a driver was needed, but otherwise had shown no interest in the work. She was an efficient, well-paid secretary to a group of doctors, and Joy had no idea she had been feeling God wanted her to leave that job and work in a missionary

organisation. It was a time when spiritual movements were
starting which were attracting much interest in evangelical
circles in Los Angeles. Virginia had heard about them —
Wycliffe Bible Translators, Missionary Aviation Fellowship,
Far East Broadcasting Company ... She wondered if she
would receive a Divine intimation that she should apply to one
of them and offer her services as a secretary. She was quite
willing to leave her comfortable position with its secure salary,
well-appointed office, interesting conventions in luxurious
hotels, to throw in her lot with one of them. But that little
set-up of Joy Ridderhof's had not crossed her mind, neither
had it occurred to Joy that Virginia might join her. So when
the two happened to meet at a wedding reception, and Virginia
enquired cheerfully, 'How's it going?' Joy's reply was spontaneous and quite unpremeditated.

'Getting on fine,' she said with a smile. 'But we sure need
you!'

That night Virginia went home with the words echoing in
her mind. 'We sure need you.' Spoken so laughingly, they were
charged with an authority of which Joy herself was quite
unaware. 'We need you ... need you ... you.'

Before going to bed that night Virginia prayed very directly.
'Lord, do you want me to go and help Joy?' She expected an
answer, though she did not know how it would come. It came
through her daily Bible reading the very next morning, as she
came to the words in Isaiah 12.3, *Therefore with joy shall ye
draw waters out of the wells of salvation.*

'With joy ...' Virginia looked at the words comprehend-
ingly. 'With Joy.' There was God's answer. It was so simple,
so direct, so convincing that she had no doubt as to Who had
spoken to her. She acted promptly. She gave in her notice and
wrote to Joy.

She had to wait a fortnight before she received a reply. Joy
wasn't accustomed to having a full-time secretary, let alone
one with such qualifications as Virginia's. She wondered what
she would give her to do, as she realised there would not be
enough office work to keep her busy. Strictly speaking, there
wasn't even an office at all — it was being fitted into a corner of

the studio they were making from the old stable, and was still unfinished. Virginia knew nothing of the earnest conversations Joy had with Ann about the unexpected offer, whether she was justified in accepting it since there was really not enough for an experienced secretary to do. But there was the evidence that Virginia's call had come from God, and eventually she received a letter from Joy, arranging that she should turn up for work on the first of April. She mounted the steps leading up to 122 Witmer Street promptly on time, like the reliable secretary she was, ready for a day at the typewriter.

Marie answered the door. Joy was in bed, she said, she'd had a very late night. When Joy appeared she led Virginia over to the studio and gave her a paint pot and brush. Would she mind painting the window frame of what was to be her office?

So commenced the first day of the first person to leave a well-paid job to become an unsalaried member of Gospel Recordings. Virginia was quite happy about it. Thirty-five years later she had no doubt as to why she was still a member. God had called her into Gospel Recordings, and God had kept her there.

4

Always a Step Ahead

'EXTRA PETROL COUPONS? For what purpose?' the official enquired coldly.

'We want to go to the Mazahua tribe in Mexico to make recordings for them,' replied Joy rather lamely. The official was unusually frigid, and she began to wonder if it would be quite as simple a matter as she had anticipated to obtain those coupons.

'And what is the purpose of these recordings?' The voice was sharp and impersonal. When she explained as briefly as she could that they were to give the Gospel to the Mazahua in their own tongue, the official's attitude became glacier-like.

'I suppose you are aware that the country is at war?' he said contemptuously. 'That the requirements of our forces must take precedence over purely personal and unnecessary journeys such as you outline? No, I cannot authorise the issue of petrol coupons to you.' Then he had an afterthought.

'What allocation of petrol is your organisation receiving?' She told him. 'Too much! Far too much for such an organisation. It will have to be reduced. Good-day, Miss Ridderhof . . .'

Joy emerged from the Petrol Office feeling thoroughly dispirited. This was the worst setback she had received since the Wycliffe Bible Translators in Mexico had approached her, expressing their desire that something should be done for the Mazahua tribe. 'It is so scattered, and it seems that the only way to reach it with the Gospel is by means of your records. If we brought some of these tribes people to Los

Angeles, would you be willing to make records in their tongue also?'

Of course she had said yes. The little studio in the back garden at Witmer Street was in full working order, and she and Ann were mastering the techniques of recording. Already they had recorded programmes in several other languages with the co-operation of foreign students and missionaries. So with bi-lingual interpreters prepared to come from Mexico she had no hesitation in responding to the W.B.T. request.

Then had come the first setback. The historical Japanese attack on Pearl Harbour had already brought the U.S.A. into the Second World War, and restrictions were tightening. When application was made to bring two or three Mazahua tribesmen from Mexico to Los Angeles, permission was refused.

'Rejoice!' said Joy. 'It's all right. God must have a purpose in it.' The challenge to her faith was crystallising into a conviction that the refusal was part of God's plan. An impression that there was a wider work for Gospel Recordings had deepened in her mind in the past few months. There had been the unexpected gift of a portable disc recorder, for instance. Surely a *portable* machine had not been intended to remain in the studio? In the apparent setback she saw God's finger pointing in a new direction. 'If the Mazahua mayn't come to us' she said 'then we will go to them.'

'We will go to them.' The call of the small tribes, the scattered, isolated groups of primitive people shrinking away from the march of civilisation into the backwoods and the deserts and the jungles had reached her. She had no idea at that time how almost innumerable they were, or to what lengths she herself would be impelled to go to find them. She was conscious, however, that beyond the Mazahua were even more inaccessible little clans and no voice would tell them in the only tongue they could understand that God loved them — unless she and her colleagues did something about it.

So she had talked it over with Ann and Virginia and the voluntary workers who came along to help, and they had all agreed she and Ann must go to Mexico. It meant leaving a heavy load of work to the others, and more than that, a new responsibility. For the house next door had fallen vacant, and Gospel Recordings was negotiating to buy it. A heavy mortgage was involved, and in faith that God would provide the money they were undertaking to pay it all off in a year. However, the immediate needs connected with the journey into Mexico loomed even larger, for it was necessary to take the recording equipment with them, and as the portable disc recorder alone weighed nearly a hundred pounds it was obvious that a large saloon car would be needed. They hadn't got one, nor the money to buy one, either. But they were confident they were moving ahead with their plans and preparations under Divine compulsion, and that a vehicle would materialise in time for them to set off on the day appointed. To obtain the necessary coupons for an extra petrol allocation for the journey had seemed a very insigificant matter, since reasonable requests were not refused, and Joy had anticipated no difficulty when she walked into the office that day. The unexpected and icy rejection of her application took her by surprise, and filled her with dismay.

The occasions when she was caught off guard and gave way to discouragement were very few, but this was one of them. She returned to Witmer Street and mounted the steps up to the house rather heavily, hoping she would meet no-one. She wanted to get to her room, so that she could think and pray alone. She must regain her spiritual equilibrium, pray through, with fasting if necessary. What had gone wrong? There were only three days to go to the date fixed for the departure to Mexico. People there were expecting them, all arrangements had been made, the recording equipment was in order. It would all be useless unless the necessary transport were forthcoming and now, even if a car miraculously arrived at the doorstep they couldn't go, simply because they had not got the necessary petrol coupons.

She knelt by her bed, prepared to spend the rest of the day, and even the night too, in prayer, seeking to find out the reason why those coupons were not given. Had they made some mistake in their plans? Were they running ahead of God?

A tap came on the door, and almost before Joy could scramble to her feet Ann walked in.

'Get ready for a shock, Joy,' she said. 'I've got something to tell you. But you'd better sit down first.' Joy obeyed.

'We've got a station wagon,' said Ann, her face aglow. 'Loaned to us for as long as we need it. A Pontiac.'

Joy gasped. 'Who's lending it to us?'

Ann mentioned the name of her doctor, an old family friend. She had gone to him for a medical check-up, and after assuring her she was quite fit to undertake journeys of several months in Mexico he asked how she planned to go there. They planned to go by car, she answered, but admitted they hadn't got the car yet.

The doctor had acted quickly. A few days before he had seen an advertisement of a Pontiac station wagon for sale. 'I expect it'll be gone by now,' he said, but put through a phone call all the same. It was still for sale! The outcome was that it was brought over to the doctor's house, and he paid for it on the spot. The owner had arranged to go to Mexico in it, but his plans had been changed, and now he was going by plane instead.

'So now it's ours for as long as we need it!' concluded Ann triumphantly. 'My doctor says he won't want to use it for months yet, so we can borrow it!'

'Isn't that wonderful!' said Joy, not quite so whole-heartedly as usual. 'But Ann ... I couldn't get the petrol coupons. The man at the Petrol Office wouldn't give them to me. And without them ...'

'Oh, the owner had already got his petrol coupons for the journey, so he offered them with the car,' replied Ann. 'We've got everything we need – car and sufficient coupons to take us right through to Mexico.'

So that was why the visit to the Petrol Office had proved unproductive! God had made the provision in His own way, and the manner of it was a further lesson to them to be prepared for the unexpected. The way of life into which they were stepping would follow no clearly defined paths nor fall into any regular pattern. It required not so much shrewd foresight as a close walk with their Guide, and a faith that would sing even when things seemed to go wrong. The duet of trial and triumph to which Joy had referred in her days in Marcala was to accompany her all her life, and since she knew that God's testings are for the purpose, not of causing us to fall but of making us strong, she could accept them cheerfully. The more acute the trial, the more rapturous the triumph.

They set out in high spirits on this their first journey abroad to make recordings, cruising along the great Pan-American Highway, twisting, climbing over mountains and through deserts to Mexico City. Their enthusiasm was subdued after several days of scouring the narrow crowded streets looking for a studio to rent, but it soared again when Joy suddenly remembered the name of a man whose brother had told her that if ever she were in Mexico City she ought to look him up. He was very interested in recording.

She traced him in the telephone directory, made the necessary explanations when she got him on the phone, and then asked if he knew of a studio they could rent.

'Why, sure! I've got a room I only use one day a week. You're welcome to use it any other time you like. Rent? Aw, nothing! It's there, and I'm not using it – glad for you to have it.'

They gasped when they saw the place. It was the most sumptuously furnished studio they had ever worked in, with heavy curtains and thick pile carpets hushing every sound from the tumultuous streets outside. Into it came the Wycliffe Bible Translators bringing bare-footed, primitive Indians, with Joy and Ann crouching hour after hour over the machine, alert and tense to capture those Indian voices. The missionaries had translated the scripts into the Mazahua language, and as the Indians read them the machine went into action, catching each sound as it fell from the lips of the strangers whose language the two recordists could neither understand nor speak. But the Indians understood. Comprehension revealed itself on their face combined with incredulity as they listened to the whole programme being played back to them, heard themselves

telling of the God in Heaven who had made all things, and who
loved them, whose Son had died for them. There in the studio
the key was being fitted into the lock that would eventually
open the door of faith to these people. The master records were
made and carefully stored, ready for the time when they could
be taken back to Los Angeles and used to press tens, hundreds,
thousands of the little discs that were eventually to find their
way back into the hearts of the tribal villages where the words
would be heard in voices that all could understand. And the
number of languages mounted slowly up, one, two, three, ten,
twenty, thirty. Joy and Ann were in Mexico for months, and
by the time they were getting ready to leave they had master
records in thirty-three languages, twenty-five of them in tribal
languages into which no part of the Scriptures had yet been
produced.

Before they returned to Los Angeles, however, there was
one thing Joy must do. She must fulfil the promise she had
made to the people of Marcala that she would return.

It was the highlight of that year of 1944 for her when once
more she was astride a little mule, going clippity-clop, clippity-
clop up the path that led to Marcala. Before she could get
inside she was met by a crowd of welcoming people, and her
body seemed too small to hold the excitement and the joy and
the love with which she saw them. There they were, smiling
and laughing and crying at once, and the eight years of
separation were swallowed up and forgotten as she went from
one to another, eagerly embracing the women in that
traditional way she had learned so easily, laughingly refraining
from embracing the men as well, so glad, so very glad, to be
with them all again. Tears sprang to their eyes and to hers too,
as they talked, and sang together, and went into the little
chapel to give thanks to God. They knew she could not remain
with them, of course. She told them of the new horizons
opening up through the use of the gramophone records, and
how it was her love for them, the people of Marcala, that had
first inspired her to produce them. Now she must return to this
task which God had committed to her. They understood, and
they let her go, though not without tears. As for Joy, she rode

away but with an invisible cord that seemed to tug at her heart, uniting her forever with those people of Marcala.

Meanwhile, in Los Angeles itself, jubilant preparations were being made for the return of Joy and Ann. No matter how much work there was to be done, it must all stop for three days, to give adequate time for the double celebration — the return of the two travellers from Mexico, and the official house-warming of 124 Witmer Street, head-quarters of Gospel Recordings! For the mortgage had all been paid off, and that within nine months, although no appeal for financial help had been made in any direction whatever. The money had just come, in small sums and large sums, sometimes from friends, sometimes from almost complete strangers. With what pride were visitors shown round the six-roomed house, what stories were told of the way furniture had been provided, and curtains, and kitchen-ware! What reports there were to give of the way the work had gone ahead, too.

Spanish recordings were being used over long wave radio in Latin America.

Records sent out to mission fields had risen to nearly twenty thousand.

Best of all, letters were produced and read telling of people hearing the Gospel for the very first time over the gramophone, and of many, here and there, coming to faith in Christ.

Reports from Joy and Ann were even more thrilling, because they had the smack of danger and adventure about them. There had been journeys off the beaten track, to villages where they were asked to preach (by interpretation) and were amazed at the response.

'Our hearts were touched by the way they hungrily grasped at every truth presented and gladly yielded themselves to the Saviour. "You must forgive us," they said, "for not knowing these things, but it is as though we were blind . . . But just give us time. We will learn if you will only help us."

'The Wycliffe translators generously took us into their own home, and were prepared to bring in their workers from the tribes, Christian tribespeople with them, each ready to make records in his own tongue. Ten-year-old Tino talked so softly we had to put cotton in his ears to raise his voice so the microphone could pick it up! But Tino, with one of the consecrated Wycliffe translators, was able to make a set of six double Gospel records in the language of his tribe, the Mazateco . . .' The stories seemed endless, and the journeyings, too, as it must have seemed on the occasion when they were held up by violent storms for twenty-three days in a little border town.

'But God had a purpose in it and gave us souls again as we worked with the three little local evangelical churches. Throughout this entire trip we were brought face to face with Ephesians 5.20, "Giving thanks always for all things to God." And we were allowed to see some of His reasons for changing our plans.'

Giving thanks always to God. That had been the mainspring of their cheerfulness when things seemed to go wrong, when funds were low, 'we travelled several weeks with only an average of four dollars between us', when the work was slow and tedious and the tribespeople were dull. 'Carmen's records had to be made in several pieces and put together afterwards, since he couldn't get through a whole one without mistakes.' And even when all the fruit of their months of record-making was threatened by official censorship, and they saw no way of bringing the four hundred master records they had made out of Mexico, Joy insisted that they must rejoice. God was still God, and He was sovereign. He had sent them to Mexico, He had provided for them in so many wonderful ways, nothing was impossible to Him. 'Rejoice in the Lord *always*. Again I say, Rejoice!' Paul had written in a Roman prison, and if he could be glad in such circumstances surely they could be glad in theirs!

The particular problem they were faced with had certainly been formidable, for it had been two-edged. The censor was insisting that before they could be taken out of the country all the master records made in Mexico must be played over to ensure they contained no subversive material. The two-edged problem lay in the irrefutable fact that there was no official in Mexico or anywhere else who understood all of the thirty-three languages that had been recorded, and that even had such a linguistic wizard been found the master records would all have been rendered useless for reproduction. If played over even once, they would be spoiled.

Praising and praying and believing that somehow or other God would find a solution to the problem they went from office to office, requesting unsuccessfully that they might be permitted to take the records out uncensored. But there in Mexico City was one man whose position was sufficiently influential, and whose sympathies were sufficiently broad, to be able to help them. He listened to the two Protestant women explaining that they wished to send records about God and Jesus to tribes of Indians who had little or no knowledge of Christianity. Joy was the spokeswoman, and as always when she started relating what God was doing in Gospel Recordings, she became more and more animated, her face lighted up from time to time into a broad smile as she exclaimed 'Wasn't that wonderful?' and the official, listening attentively, quietly nodded his head. 'I'll see you get the necessary papers,' he said when she had finished and after he had put through a long distance phone call, and seen to one or two other matters relating to the affair, he provided them with the official documents they needed. Over the border they went, unimpeded, back into the United States with four hundred master records safely stored in the back of the station wagon.

The new era in Gospel Recordings had begun – the era of the field recordists.

*   *   *

It was one thing to arrive triumphantly home from Mexico with some four hundred master records in thirty-odd languages to be carefully stored in the studio. It was quite another thing to get them on to stampers that would press out the discs that could be sent back to the tribes waiting for them. That part of the process involved many phone calls to factories which did that sort of thing, many delays, many visits to collect the precious discs only to be told that the order had not been completed yet. And even when the piles of gramophone records were eventually delivered, and labelled, and packed, and the shipping forms filled in, and the boxes delivered to the appropriate departments and the bills paid, one couldn't help realising that unless the tribes for which the records had been prepared happened to possess gramophones – gramophones that worked – the whole exercise from first to last was so much wasted effort.

The collecting and repairing of old gramophones to be given away with the records when necessary had been back-room work going on since 1939. Now, in 1945, it was part of the unromantic, inner workings of Gospel Recordings, and what with the recording machinery which had a knack of going wrong at inconvenient moments, and occasions when heavy cases had to be lugged about, the Gospel Recordings team of women found themselves talking about their need of a man – a man who knew enough about electrical equipment to do the repairs that were running away with so much money as experts were brought in, and who would also do some of the heavy work that made women so breathless.

For apart from Lloyd Olson who saw to the shipping of records, the staff was still composed of women. Ann's niece, Doris, was in the work now. Her call to it had come, as had Virginia Miller's, through an unpremeditated remark of Joy's when, in bed in an adjoining room one night Joy had suddenly called out laughingly, 'Doris, why don't you come into Gospel Recordings?' She went sound asleep after that, but Doris spent a sleepless night.

Why not join Gospel Recordings? The chief reason against it, from Doris' point of view, was that it was just what she wanted to do, and she was afraid of following her own inclination. As she thought and prayed through the dark hours of the night, however, she became aware that a gracious and loving Heavenly Father was planning to give her her heart's desire. The very next day she wrote and told her mother that she would be joining Ann and Joy in their work.

'Doris? What can she do?' asked someone sceptically when the news got round, but Joy was jubilant, asserting that if God had called Doris into G.R. He had something for her to do. Doris was willing for anything, and though she had been trained as a teacher, got off to a good start in the office. But when it came to electronics and mechanics and lifting heavy machinery, she was no better than the rest of them. The need for a masculine arm and a man's brain was increasingly evident.

The team talked about the sort of man they needed.

'He needs to be young and strong,' they said to each other. 'And willing to do any type of work, however hard and menial.'

'Good-natured and tolerant, too,' added one. 'Able to get along with a bunch of women.'

'We might put an advertisement in the papers specifying these requirements,' the banter continued. 'And we'd better explain that no salary will be paid, the applicant must be prepared to work full time and pay all his own expenses, including board.'

They put no advertisement in a paper, but they made their request, more soberly, to the God of Heaven, and the answer they received surpassed all their expectations. A blond youth measuring six foot three inches arrived at the door of the studio in the back garden one day, announcing that he was Herman Dyk, and he had come to see if there was anything he could do to help them. He had heard about them in Montana, one thousand miles away, and felt God wanted him to join them.

When Joy recovered from her surprise she welcomed him, but explained the unusual financial basis on which the work was run, rather apologetically pointing out that there was no salary attached to the job, though there was plenty of hard work. Herman was not disturbed. The only mention he made of money was to enquire whether he might be permitted to make a donation. As for work, he was used to it, and set about shouldering heavy machinery and bales of goods with a cheerful grin. The most remarkable thing, however, was that he seemed to know all about wires and wheels, balance and minute measurements, so that obstinate machines started whirring and spinning under his touch. The repairs that had been running away with so much money and so much time were now attended to on the spot, in an afternoon. 'Herman has fixed it!' the team said wonderingly until they got used to it, when they said instead, with carefree confidence, 'Herman will fix it!'

For Herman, it transpired, was an experienced electronics technician.

He was not the only answer to Joy's prayers for a man who knew about machinery, although it was several months before she realised it. When Albert R. Rethey was brought along by a friend of his to see this remarkable little organisation that was producing records in all sorts of languages, Joy merely saw a tall man with a grave smile who bowed to her courteously and listened with respectful interest to what she told him. It was all new to him, this down-to-earth enthusiasm for sending the Gospel in the shape of gramophone records to people of whom he had never heard. But then, everything about the Gospel was new to Albert R. Rethey. He had attended a church where the theory of evolution was taught and accepted, and it wasn't until he heard and saw Dr. Moon of Facts and Faith Films giving lectures which included something about wire recording (which happened to be in his line) that he realised there was any other point of view. Then, some time later, he had listened in to some radio programmes containing Bible studies, and this had led him to study the Bible for himself. In middle life, he had just received the Kingdom of God with the simplicity of a little child, and as a little child he was entering into the affairs of that Kingdom. It was gratifying to learn that those affairs sometimes even led to mechanical matters such as he was accustomed to, for he happened to hold a unique position as Technical Consultant in Consolidated Steel, at that time the largest steel firm on the west coast of America.

He had learned the various skills required to carry him to the top the hard way, starting from the time when his father bought a business, told Al how to produce dry cell batteries for ignition purposes, and left him to it. His basic knowledge of chemistry was gained there. Later he went to work for

Consolidated Steel, and was loaned to Hollywood's Metro Goldwyn Meyer to help design equipment for process photography whereby abnormal effects were obtained of dramatic, hair-raising accidents. Mobile action cameras mounted on platforms with wheels occupied his attention for a while, and here he gained his expertise in mechanical construction. Then his firm sent him to Texas, where a ship building plant was being established. As expeditor he knew just where to obtain the heavy material necessary, castings weighing 15 tons and all. There really wasn't very much about mechanics generally that Albert R. Rethey did not know.

Joy might have been expected to be rather over-awed that such a person should come to see her amateur set-up, but she did not even know who he was. She merely saw in his visit an opportunity to discuss something that was puzzling her. She had recently bought a cutting lathe for cutting grooves in discs. She had got it cheap because the owner told her it wasn't working too well, so he was willing to let it go at $150, less than one tenth of its original price. To Joy $150 was quite a lot of money, but she felt convinced she should get the lathe, so she bought it.

The problem about it was that, as the owner had admitted, it wasn't working well. In fact, it wasn't really working at all, and Joy, who had rejoiced at having enough money to buy it was now rejoicing because although it didn't work God must have had a purpose in prompting her to buy it, and maybe the arrival of Mr. Rethey had something to do with it.

So it proved. Mr. Rethey asked if he might look at the lathe. As it happened it was one he himself had invented, though he did not mention it. Within minutes he had extracted a small steel mechanism about two inches long which he held up for her to see.

'This reduction gear for the screw drive is too small for your purpose,' he said. 'But there's nothing much to it. We can easily replace it, and then the lathe will work perfectly.' It was as easy as that! Joy gasped. What seemed like a mechanical miracle was performed which set the lathe working and Joy rejoicing. She had known God had a purpose in her buying that lathe . . . !

There was a deeper purpose than the restoration of a cutting lathe, though, for it brought Al Rethey into the work. He came along once or twice a week after that first visit to see if there was any way in which he could help. Sometimes Joy did not know what to do with him, and often he was seen descending the steps to his sumptuous big Buick laden with parcels for mailing, or going off to pick up records being pressed in some out of the way little commercial plant. But when Lloyd Olson set about re-constructing the basement for record storage, Albert R. Rethey knew all about supports for the under structure, and what is more he knew where to get them. Joy beamed with appreciation.

The simplicity and the sincerity of it all spoke to the guileless man. He felt at home here, quietly marvelled at the reports that came in telling of people being transformed through what they heard on the records, and decided that this was a work worth giving the rest of his life to. When Consolidated Steel was bought out by the largest steel corporation in the United States, he decided he would not accept a position in the new firm, but instead would retire and give his services to Gospel Recordings.

No-one could have foreseen in 1946 what the two men who came so unobtrusively into the work were to mean to it in the years to come. At that time there was no serious expectation of Gospel Recordings having its own factory and thereby being able to dispense with the uncèrtain and expensive services of commercial firms for the production of records. The work had already extended beyond anything Joy had envisaged. It seemed as though the Lord was always a step ahead. At times she scarcely knew how to keep up with Him. There was only one way to do it, as far as she could see, and she amazed her colleagues by announcing that everybody at G.R. should stop working on Wednesdays, and spend the day together in praying and praising God instead. She was in the State of Washington at the time, to speak at a few meetings that had been arranged, and while there attended a prayer conference.

'The speaker stressed prayer more than anyone I had ever heard. "In everything by prayer with thanksgiving make your requests known unto God." We all know the injunctions to prayer in the Word of God. "Pray without ceasing." This made a deep impression on me linking up in my memory my early teaching at the Columbia Bible School where I had taken my training. It was the continual stress, "rejoicing and prayer". I not only was taught but saw it practised. My years on the mission field bore it out as I never forgot the importance of prayer. But now I was in a new undertaking. Yes, prayer must be the most important part of it, if we want the blessing of the Lord in its fulness.'

So she put through that phone call to Gospel Recordings Inc. in Los Angeles. 'How are things going?' she enquired. 'We're too busy – we can't get through,' was the reply.

'Take a day off for prayer,' she said. It was not a suggestion, it was an instruction.

The decree was received with some dismay at Witmer Street.

'A whole day out for prayer! We've got too much work to do already, how will we ever get through it?'

'Does she mean *every* Wednesday?'

'Things will just get right on top of us ...'

Joy, however, had forestalled all such arguments by saying, 'You can't do the work anyway, so you might just as well pray about it and get the Lord to help you.'

It did not occur to any of them to question her right to issue such instructions, so they started spending Wednesdays in prayer and singing and telling each other of the encouragements the Lord had given them through their Bible readings, and in their personal lives. Not many weeks had passed before any doubts were dissolved about the wisdom of the unusual allocation of a complete working day. Their output had not been reduced at all. In fact, they seemed to get through more quickly. Virginia, who had a way of defining things clearly, put it like this,

'Prayer brings resistance from the natural man, but once that's been overcome the increase of inward stability, of assurance, gives ability for the work. In addition, things happen outside that can't be accounted for, but which make things run more smoothly.'

It was about the same time that Joy introduced the policy of providing all gramophone records without charge. The Gospel was free, and the records should be free too. In so many cases the people who needed them most were the ones who could not afford to buy them. 'We'll give all the records away for nothing.' Not surprisingly the cautious-minded raised their eyebrows at this reckless abandoning of a legitimate source of income, but Joy was adamant. Quite apart from the spiritual principle involved, it would save a lot of time and effort expended in keeping accounts, sending out estimates and dealing with the Tax Office.

At the end of the financial year their accountant admitted that he had looked with amazement at the balancing of accounts each month. The output of records had increased by nearly double, yet no debts were incurred.

There had been a few times when faith was tested as word went round the departments that there was not sufficient money in hand to pay any more bills, and that nothing more might be bought, however urgent the need. That warning had always resulted in more stringent economies and an increased intensity of prayer. It was a sobering thing to see stacks of records packed and ready for shipping piled up on the floor because there wasn't the money in hand to dispatch them. Rejoicing was all the more fervent when money flowed in again, and the piles of records disappeared. In those early days principles were being laid down that were the outcome of a faith that was venturing, finding encouragement at every step, though not without trials.

By this time Joy and Ann were preparing for another recording trip. This time they were going to the extreme north, the uttermost part of the American continent, to that remote part of United States territory that straddled the Arctic circle. They were planning to travel by car up the newly opened Alaska Highway.

Going to Alaska! Areas ice bound for months on end; vast

stretches of desolate wilderness; bitter winds howling across the snow; packs of wolves roaming; drunkenness rife in the scattered towns and lumber camps. Even if there were petrol stations every hundred miles along the Highway, what if the car broke down midway? It simply was not right for two women to travel alone up there.

If only they had a young man to go with them it would be different. It would be safer then. But to go without a man . . . !

Joy knew what was being said, of course, and smiled as one day she came in her reading in Isaiah to the words,

Even the youths shall faint and be weary, and the young men shall utterly fall.

No young men it seemed had felt any urge to make a recording trip to Alaska to provide the Words of life in their own tongues to the tribes of Indian aboriginals and Eskimos cut off for months in their little igloos or heavy skin wigwams. But if the urge had come to her and to Ann, how could they withstand it? She read on, and almost laughed aloud with exultation,

But they that wait upon the Lord shall renew their strength; they shall mount up with wings as eagles; they shall run and not be weary, they shall walk and not faint.

Those promises were not to men only. The promises were to whoever waited upon the Lord, men or women. She and Ann could be assured of the vigour they would need, provided they fulfilled the condition. So the day came when they packed their luggage into the car, Al Rethey and Herman loaded the heavy recording material into the back, and amid a chorus of 'Goodbye and God bless you' they set off on the four thousand mile journey that would take them to the uttermost part.

Al Rethey and Herman looked after them reflectively, then returned to their machines. They had their own affairs to see to, and their own consciousness of an inward urge.

'We ought to have our own record pressing machine,' they agreed. 'It would save hundreds, thousands of dollars if we could press our own records. And what's more, we would have the service when we wanted it — no waiting till next week or next month to fulfil the urgent orders.'

Those constant delays in getting the records pressed and sent back to the little tribes off the beaten track were having one good effect in Gospel Recordings. They were increasing the sense of urgency, the inward pressure to get on with the task. When inward pressure is strong enough, as with steam suppressed, something begins to move.

'We'll have to get a pressing machine made,' said Al Rethey. 'Made to our own design, to suit our requirements.' He settled down to working on plans that involved hydraulics and heavy machinery, but his mind was moving in another direction, too, following Joy and Ann up the Alaskan Highway. 'That disc recording machine – terribly heavy for women to have to handle, lugging it in and out of the back of the car.' He talked it over with Herman.

'There's this new method of recording with tape instead of discs. Lighter and easier to handle. What they need is a tape recording machine that they can take around with them.'

Pity they hadn't got one for this trip ... They were obtainable, if only there was the money to pay for them ... But even the best of them were quite heavy ...

'What they need is something really light, easy for women to carry,' the men agreed. 'There's nothing else for it. We'll have to try to make one ourselves.'

When Joy and her team had prayed for a man it had not occurred to them to ask for an inventor. It had not occurred to them that they needed one. They saw no farther than having someone who could do repairs and lift heavy burdens.

But the Lord was always a step ahead.

5

Golden Moments

WHEN JOY CAME to review the five months spent on the Alaskan trip, she realised that the deepest impression made on her had been through a casual remark in the course of conversation on the very first day they arrived in the Copper River Indian Valley. The surprising thing was that the casual remark had nothing whatever to do with Alaska.

The young American missionary couple living in the Valley had already started planning the recording programme. They knew how short would be the brilliant summer when wild flowers added their vivid colours to the rich green that ran like a carpet to the base of the mountains that were forever capped with snow. Right now they were laying in stores of food and logs in preparation for the biting cold of the long grey winter. Opportunities for travel must be grasped quickly, they insisted, and they had maps and information ready for inspection, while names like Kotzebue and Kuskokiwin, Diomede and Malemute slipped readily off their tongues, and a dozen more besides. Then suddenly, in the midst of it all, a memory had flashed something to the surface of young Clark's mind.

'Talking of tribal languages, Miss Ridderhof,' he had said. 'There are scores and scores of different groups in the Philippine Islands. I was there in the war, and saw some of them. All different, all speaking their own language – and most of them without the least knowledge of the Gospel. Any amount of tribes there . . .'

He had turned back to the map of Alaska then, eager to get

on with the task on hand. He pointed to Hudson Bay and Fish River, indicated the places where they would have to go to get recordings, and the places where there were bi-lingual Indian Eskimos who could be persuaded to come to them. These were the people he was responsible for. The tribes of the Philippines subsided into the past, where as far as he was concerned they belonged, and he was back again in the present, in Alaska, where God had called him.

But for Joy it was different. Her eyes followed his finger as he pointed here and there, and her mind fastened on the information and plans while Ann, as usual, rapidly jotted them in her notebook. But that night when she crawled into her sleeping bag on the front seat of the Pontiac parked beside the Clarks' little log cabin, it was of the palm-fringed islands of the Pacific that she found herself thinking.

The Philippines. The great archipelago stretching like a chaplet of jewels off the mainland of Asia had been headline news during the Second World War, when the United States of America was pitchforked into action by the Japanese undeclared aerial attack on Manila. Descriptions of the islands, of the loyalty of the people to the *Americanos* who had promised to return, the stories of bridgeheads made by the gallantry and courage of the U.S. Marines, the battles in the air, on the sea, on the land, the ultimate victory and the delirious joy of the liberated islanders had all made stirring reading. Joy, like the rest of her nation, had warmed towards the people of the Philippines. And there, hidden in the mountains and the jungles and the lovely, far-off beaches, were tribes, scores of them, who were waiting to hear that God loved them, waiting to be released from the fear of evil spirits and death that held them in bondage.

It was as though a Divine searchlight had flashed suddenly upon a far distant scene, focussing her attention momentarily on something she hadn't known was there, but which she could now never forget. Throughout the varied experiences of the Alaskan trip, which included journeying by train, steamer, fishing boat and aeroplane, recording in such unusual places as a Russian cemetery and Indian wigwams, the thought of the tribes of the Philippines remained in her mind, ready to rise to the surface the moment it was undisturbed by other matters.

The Alaskan recording trip went well from the first. On the very day Joy and Ann left Los Angeles they decided suddenly that they would take advantage of an offer made by a friend to obtain for them one of the new portable tape recording machines that were just on the market. They had no money to pay for it, but realising how much more they would be able to accomplish if they could travel light they believed God would provide it when the time came. They'd leave it to Him. They put through a telephone call and ordered one. They mentioned it to no-one, not even at places where they were invited to speak about the work, but by the time they reached the Canadian border, where they had arranged to pick up the machine, they had received all they needed to clear the account.

The four thousand mile journey was accomplished without so much as a punctured tyre, and as they sped along over the Alaskan Highway they exclaimed, 'What a marvellous feat of engineering it is!' Joy wrote of it later, for it had provided her with an analogy which inspired and challenged her.

'As we rode along this gravel-covered road which spanned thousands of miles through a vast wilderness and jungle, we read about its construction. Some engineers drew the blueprints, some men handled the trucks, others worked with their shovels, cooks prepared food in make-shift kitchens, nurses and doctors attended the wounds and insect bites of labourers, aviators and trucks brought supplies from distant markets, carpenters prepared temporary shelters for workmen, officials and labourers together sweltered or froze as the case might be, working out of doors in this place of extreme temperatures. The struggles and the dangers were numerous. Wild animals, pests, mire and desolation all had their part in hampering the progress of the road. Money was constantly being supplied from the citizens of our country. The purpose was to provide a highway for military advance . . .

'They had a great incentive before them and the time was short. They pushed ahead through every obstacle, counting not the cost, with the result that a way was made where there was no way — a highway in the wilderness, and goes on record as having been one of the greatest engineering accomplishments in such a short period of time.'

In the spiritual realm, this was what she was to do — to carve a highway for God in regions and among peoples who had not yet heard of His salvation. She saw the task was not hers alone. Each varied activity played an indispensable part. Her unqualified appreciation of what others did in the less prominent positions in Gospel Recordings, the workers in studio and office and factory, had the effect of knitting them into a team in which each was conscious of making a distinctive contribution. They were in it together, and the steadily mounting number of new languages captured and records shipped farther and farther afield were achievements in which they all had a share.

The shipping of records had by this time extended far beyond the American continent. With the end of the war, new and unthought-of opportunities began to present themselves. In China particularly the door stood wide open for evangelism, and reports came in of the records being played over public address systems to hundreds of thousands. It had been simple to obtain recordings in the Chinese dialects, but who would have thought it possible to send records in the Lisu tribal language to the far-away mountains bordering on Burma? The arrival in Los Angeles of two missionaries who had been working among those colourful people had made it a reality. And since colleges in the U.S.A. were now receiving Asians from lands made free at last, Joy and Ann spent months visiting them after the Alaskan trip to make recordings in tongues that would be understood in such remote places as the borders of Tibet and the foothills of the Himalayas. They had captured twenty-one languages in Alaska, and in the year following their return sixty-six more were added, bringing the total up to nearly two hundred.

So they came to the tenth year of Gospel Recordings, and the fact did not pass unnoticed. The event must be celebrated in a fitting manner, that a spiritual Ebenezer might be raised, and credit given where it was due. 'Hitherto hath the Lord helped us.' Let all know that what had been achieved was due to His help, His provision, His guidance. Let all work stop for a week, that we may rejoice in His goodness, and share it with others! Open house for all comers, and a series of meetings at which the speaker shall be one who knows how to draw deep, satisfying nourishment from the Word of God! What better way to celebrate?

For Joy it was the highlight of the year, that week in June when Dr. McQuilkin again came to Los Angeles to conduct a series of meetings on the deepening of the spiritual life, when with her friends she was refreshed and inspired, and when the wonderful things God was doing through the little records were recounted amid prayers and praises.

There was something new to rejoice in at home, too. Albert Rethey and Herman Dyk had produced Gospel Recordings' own record pressing machine, housed in a room lent to them in Hollywood, where teams of voluntary workers could go by night as well as by day to fulfil urgent orders. Now the two men were turning their attention to the matter of making brand-new gramophones, easy to handle and light to transport, to replace the miscellaneous collection of patched-up old machines.

More full-time workers had joined the staff – a charming young musician for whom Herman Dyk gladly sacrificed his single status; one of Ann's older sisters; a secretary from Illinois trained in a lawyer's office; and Sanna Morrison Barlow from Tennessee, whose slow southern drawl and courteous southern manners marked her out as an aristocrat among the heterogeneous company bustling around in Witmer Street.

It was admitted in secret that they didn't quite know where Sanna would fit in. She was willing to try her hand at anything, but to see her standing near the kitchen sink with a bewildered smile on her face, obviously without a clue as to how to set about washing up the pile of dishes and saucepans that had accumulated there, made it evident that she knew nothing at all about doing household chores. And as she had been trained neither as teacher, nurse nor secretary, knew nothing about mechanics, and had little outlet for her social accomplishments or Bible teaching ability, there were those who wondered how long she would be able to stand the work-a-day world of Gospel Recordings.

But underneath the gentle, diffident exterior was the re-silience of supple steel. Perhaps Joy recognised it. Perhaps she was drawn to Sanna because, like herself, she was a graduate of the beloved Columbia Bible College. Perhaps she felt a personal responsibility for one who was not finding a niche in the work in Los Angeles.

Perhaps she herself did not really know why she decided to teach Sanna the rudiments of recording, by taking her on a quick recording trip through the Pacific North-west, across Indian reservations into Canada. When an instinct which she did not spend time in analysing but had learned to recognise moved her to a certain course of action, she obeyed it confidently. Her colleagues eventually ceased to be surprised at what she did. Things always seemed to work out all right.

Taking Sanna on that recording trip certainly turned out all right, for Sanna, as much by prayer and perseverance as by any innate ability, developed the qualities required to make a first-class recordist. But on that trip she learned more than techniques with a tape recorder. She got a close-up view of what living by faith in God's supplies meant. Joy never took money from Gospel Recordings funds to finance her trips, nor did she take any for personal expenditure. Neither did she talk about the matter to others. But her companion in travel could not fail to observe that when she opened her purse there were times when a thoughtful expression came over her face, and she changed her plans, or after carefully enquiring the price of something that seemed essential for her work, she decided not to buy it. Joy might be the Director of a growing organisation that was receiving a good deal of financial support from generous donors, but she did not behave as one who could draw on a substantial bank balance. Money evidently came to her from unexpected sources, for the arrival of letters often resulted in a purse that suddenly bulged again, and an exclamation from Joy of 'Praise the Lord! Isn't that wonderful — just what we were needing...!' Sanna, quick to observe, soon realised why there was delay in arranging for journeys that obviously had to be taken, and why there were times when sudden decisions were made to move at what appeared to be the last minute. The money had only just arrived — 'just the right amount, the Lord knew exactly what we needed ...'

Joy's financial experiences that autumn seemed to Sanna, who was of a picturesque turn of mind and steeped in Scripture, like a range of mountains and hills looming up which one by one 'skipped aside like lambs' and 'broke forth into singing'. By this time the journey to the Philippines was Joy's over-riding consideration, for the insistent inner call of those islands could not be denied. Arrangements were being made for her to board the S.S. *McKinley* with Ann at the end of October, to set off on their first journey across the Pacific. But on the day they were due to go and get their passports they both realised they hadn't the necessary nine dollars required to pay for them. Nine dollars is a small sum compared with $485, the price of each ticket, but it is an enormous amount if you don't happen to have it when obtaining your passport depends on it. It was what was called a 'pocketbook emergency', and Joy saw it as a cause for rejoicing, because now they would see what God would do!

By the afternoon the money was in hand, and they got their passports.

Two months later, when twenty dollars were required for visas, the same sort of thing happened. The little hills had skipped aside like lambs, Sanna noted, but what of the mountain of that $485 apiece for the tickets? When the time came for a down payment there was another supply that came in at the last moment. But the whole price must be paid soon, and no-one knew where it was coming from.

It came, a few days before the S.S. *McKinley* was due to sail, from a lady who had intimated out of the blue that she wanted to pay for the two passages to the Philippines.

The story is easily told in retrospect, but it was not so easy to live through. Hills and mountains of financial shortage were not the only obstacles that had loomed up in those weeks in the autumn of 1948. An indefinable pall had been gathering over the Gospel Recordings compound, although Joy was not conscious of it until she returned from the north-west. Then it dawned on her that the cheerful spirit had departed from the headquarters in Witmer Street, that there were glum silences at meals, that there was an undercurrent of critical murmuring. There were bales of records packed and ready, but held up because there was not the money in hand to pay the lading charges. There were regular accounts, usually paid so promptly, still waiting to be settled. But these matters were of secondary importance compared to the evident lack of harmony among the staff and voluntary workers.

No-one was to blame. The discontent did not stem from any one person or from some deep-seated difference of opinion. It had come like the effects of food that has been poisoned, no-one knows how, and all were in some way affected. In a way, it was not surprising, and Joy knew it. She and Ann were about to embark on something that would be an invasion of the Evil One's territory, and this was his way of ambushing them. They couldn't expect such a move as they were contemplating to go unchallenged. It was almost reassuring, in fact, and Joy did not fail to give thanks for everything, even Satan's subtleties that were to be unmasked! But she knew she could not leave it there. The situation had to be faced, and she faced it first on her knees before God, then openly at the weekly day of prayer.

'If . . . thy brother hath ought against thee; leave thy gift before the altar, and go, first be reconciled to thy brother . . .'

First be reconciled to thy brother. The instruction was inescapable, and everyone acknowledged it. There could be no real praise, no sincere prayer for blessing on others until it had been carried out. On Wednesday, the nineteenth of October, 1948, the Gospel Recordings prayer day started with rather broken confession, and was followed by quiet conversations in which tears were very close to the surface, until gradually the tension was eased, and the day ended in an atmosphere, not so much of buoyant praise as of children who are tired, but at peace.

The ominous mountain had been scaled, and the path was smooth and sunny once more. The very next day gifts started flowing in again. The bills were paid, the records shipped, and Joy, who had paid into the depleted treasury all the money that she had, was persuaded to take it back. Ten days later she and Ann boarded the liner at San Francisco, and set off across the Pacific for the Philippines.

It hadn't occurred to her, or anyone else, that no-one in Manila was expecting them.

*   *   *

It occurred to her when they were on the liner, though, and to Ann also. As always, especially when they had time on their hands, they spent hours together in prayer, and now, drawing nearer to their destination, they gave voice to their inner questions. If there's no-one on the dock to meet us . . .

What shall we do?

Where shall we go?

How shall we cope with all our baggage?

What if they demand more money for importing it than we've got?

Lord, guide us. Undertake for us. We praise Thee! We know Thou wilt see us through!

*   *   *

There are some moments that glow in a flat recital of events like gold caught in a ray of sunlight. The moment in which Robert Bowman in his office at the Far East Broadcasting Company learned in a letter just in from Virginia Miller that Joy Ridderhof and Ann Sherwood were due to arrive on S.S. *McKinley* in Manila that very day was such a one. He had his usual full programme confronting him, and he might well have decided it was too late to do anything about meeting them now. They weren't expecting him, that was certain, since he'd only just heard about it. But what happened in that moment was that he stopped in his tracks, put everything else out of his mind, waited only long enough to put through a phone call to enquire where and when the liner was due to berth, then hurried down to his car and hurtled the seven miles into Manila to arrive in time to be on the dock, waving his hat in greeting, as the vessel drew alongside. He dealt with all customs regulations on their behalf, got their equipment through free of duty, then whisked them off through the muddy streets of war-battered Manila, teeming with jeeps and people, stalls and sewage water, out to the twelve-acred estate which the F.E.B.C. and F.E.B.I.A.S.* had turned into a beautiful, park-like area where studios and bungalows, engine room and transmitter lay among well-kept lawns, flower beds and mango trees.

'Your headquarters while you're in the Philippines,' they were told. 'Anything we can do to help you, just let us know
. . .'

So they arrived in the Philippines. Throughout the whole of their adventurous times in those mountainous islands rising out of the sea, the realisation that they had this place of refuge to return to provided an undergirding reassurance. But it was their base only — the real work for which they had come lay in far different surroundings and conditions. And they must make their way there alone.

'I never in my life faced such a complete enigma as this; it has been like a tangle and a smoke screen as far as our seeing the next step,' wrote Joy a few days after their arrival. 'But I never felt more at rest . . . God knows what He is doing. I do get a bit restless in delays, but even they are clear indications of His will. We need such wisdom in taking steps. Shall we go in this direction or that?'

She and Ann spent hours in prayer as they went over the possibilities before them. Should they make a start in the island of Mindanao, far to the south, where the Christian and Missionary Alliance workers were ready to welcome them and provide all transport? Or would it be better to go to the long slender island of Palawan that pointed like an arrow towards Indonesia? A missionary couple was eagerly awaiting them

*Far East Bible Institute and Seminary.

there, though they lived in a remote region, difficult of access. There were known to be many tribal groups in the mountains of Mindoro, an island comparatively near. But no missionaries were there at all, and how would they get started without help?

The fourth possibility was the pagan country right there in Luzon, up in Mountain Province, with Lubuagan in the centre. They had the way pointed out and described on a map in the Institute of Science of the University of the Philippines, and viewed with alarm the prospect of driving along the treacherous trail up the Chico River Canyon. It was quite a relief, at that moment, to remember that as they had no car, they couldn't go anyway. And as the Huk guerillas, Communist inspired, were making the area increasingly dangerous, Joy had almost made up her mind that the best place to start their recording travels would be in southern Mindanao, where transport was laid on and missionaries were ready to help them. She started studying the map of Mindanao, when a chance remark brought her to an abrupt halt.

'The road to Lubuagan is impassable about two thirds of the year. There's a lot of rain up there, resulting in frequent landslides. The only time you can count on most of the interior roads being passable is in the dry season.'

'And when is the dry season?' Joy enquired.

'Now!' was the reply.

Now! So that was it. Now — or not until this time next year! A start must be made as soon as possible up the long long road that led to Lubuagan. The difficulty was that with all their recording equipment and personal baggage they'd need a car and they couldn't afford to buy or even hire one.

'If we really need it, God will give it to us,' thought Joy with an upsurge of faith, and found herself saying laughingly,

'If you see a car delivered to this place in the next few days, don't refuse it. We've put in an order for one.' Her companions laughed with her. They knew what she meant, even if they did not share her faith.

A week later she had the car. It was lent by a missionary who told her, 'God wants me to let you have my car.' When she protested that he needed it himself, he replied firmly, 'You have nothing to say about it. I am giving it to God to use for your recording trip.'

That was another golden moment. There were to be many more, lighting up long periods of delay and frustration, hardship and perplexity, for they had embarked on an enterprise far more hazardous than they had ever imagined.

Early on December 9th, they set out on their first journey to get recordings, travelling through Huk guerilla territory to the mountain resort of Baguio. They arrived after dusk, and did not know where to go. But less than half an hour after arriving in the strange city Joy found herself excitedly hugging an old friend, a member of the Southern Baptists. She and her family had just arrived from China, which was succumbing to Communism.

There were no problems as to where they could stay in Baguio after that, nor where they could meet the people who could put them on the track of the tribal groups they wanted to reach. There were many missionaries in Baguio. Everything went well, in fact – except the one thing they had come to do.

They could not make recordings. When it came to that aspect of their visit, everything seemed to go wrong. The generator produced fluctuating current. They tried out their volt meter, but could not gauge volume because the Echo-tape indicator was not working. They discovered they needed a convertor. When they obtained one and tried it, it blew out completely. It was not for 125 watts. Their days were spent going round the shops in Baguio, looking for equipment no-one seemed to stock. When they found it, something else went wrong. The generator would not start ... The microphone was too sensitive, so that aspirates resulted in a minor explosion. In the middle of it all Joy went down with an attack of amoebic dysentery and flu.

After eleven days in Baguio they had made only one record, and after nineteen days they decided the only thing to do was to return to Manila and get their recording equipment and instruments thoroughly overhauled.

It was a humbling experience. Joy remembered the letter she had written before leaving Manila, triumphantly asserting her confidence that the promises she had taken hold of would be fulfilled in the way she expected.

'The mountains shall break forth before us into singing. (Isa. 55.12). The sea will flee before us, and the little hills will skip like lambs. Revolutionaries will disappear, climate will change, our bodies will be strengthened, and we will stand and laugh as we see it, saying with the Psalmist, "What ailed thee ... Ye mountains, that ye skipped like rams ... ?"'

And now, here were she and Ann returning to Manila after nearly three weeks with next to nothing accomplished, and equipment that would not work.

'Well, one thing is certain,' she said to Ann. 'We must rejoice! We can't afford not to!' It seemed the only spiritual weapon left to them in the face of so much defeat. If they ceased to believe that God was working with them in the midst of all the difficulties, they might as well go back to Los Angeles. Her mind was soaked in the Scriptures, however, and she remembered the occasion when King Jehoshaphat actually appointed *singers*, not soldiers, to go before the army,

> *And when they began to sing and to praise, the Lord set ambushments against the children of Ammon, Moab and Mount Seir, which were come up against Judah; and they were smitten ...*

'And what's more, there was so much spoil that it took Jehoshaphat and his people three days to gather it all!' They went back to the F.E.B.C. compound which was their home in the Philippines, and true to their word, 'anything we can do to help you, just let us know', the F.E.B.C. technicians worked on the machines, and by midnight on the second day had discovered the last obstinate little mechanical fault. At six-thirty next morning Joy and Ann were on the road to Baguio again, and two days later reported exultantly — 'January 2. Made ten records!' The machine was working perfectly and they had started at last.

The machine broke down again, later on. Throughout the whole of their year in the Philippines they had to contend with mechanical problems when for one reason or another the machine on which everything depended refused to perform its function. Mechanical failures as well as mosquito bites attended their way.

The human mechanism proved equally unpredictable, too — particularly Joy's. Time and again she battled unsuccessfully with all the medicines she knew against constantly recurring bouts of dysentery and malaria, ending up on her bed while Ann sturdily took over. On one occasion, arriving in a town among the rice terraces of north Luzon, she heard a voice which she scarcely recognised as her own admitting, 'Ann. I am sick. Terribly sick.' She knew she would have to give in — she could fight against her weariness and pain no longer.

They had found a little hotel where they could stay, and for the next twelve days Joy did little else but sleep and take medicine

'These are some of the medicines I have submitted myself to in the last twelve days: streptolin (for amoeba), sulpha, aspirin, injections, quinine injections, aralen and kerosene,' she wrote to the Gospel Recordings team in Los Angeles. 'So please don't say "Take care of yourself!" '

She wrote cheerfully enough, but inwardly she was passing through one of the worst attacks of depression she had encountered. This particular illness — she had had it before! In Honduras. Her mind went back, again and again, to those last weeks in Marcala, when she had been feeling just as she felt now. She remembered the warning her friend had given her, 'You'd better go back home. You ought to see a doctor. If you don't you'll crack up completely. Something could be happening that would affect your health for the rest of your life . . .'

Her friend had been right, and she had followed her advice. Even so, what had been the outcome? Ill for three years — most of the time a semi-invalid. And now, another voice seemed to be whispering to her,

'This is the end of your Philippines recordings. You'll have to give up and go home. Remember Honduras? You stayed too long, and you never got back. This is the finish. You're a quarter of the way through what you had planned in the Philippines, and you'll have to leave it at that . . .'

But Joy was not prepared to leave it at that. There had been the ring of Divine authority in her friend's voice in Honduras, but this discouraging inner reasoning was different. She did not like the tone of that voice! It did not sound like her Master's. She and Ann had just been reading together in the book of Daniel, and she remembered that even a heathen king had said of God, 'He is the living God, and steadfast for ever ... He delivereth and rescueth, and He worketh signs and wonders. He is Daniel's God.' He was Joy Ridderhof's God too, she reaffirmed inwardly, and decided that although she was feeling so ill she and Ann would complete the last assignment in Luzon island before moving on. She was not so much expecting God to heal her suddenly as to give her the strength to go through. So they set off for the province of Abra.

It proved to be the way of deliverance. In the first place, an apparently chance meeting with a young Filipino from Manila whom they knew, and who was returning home to Abra, meant that the whole burden of driving and managing affairs was taken from Ann's weary shoulders. Then, on arrival, friends in the Mennonite Social Mission were in possession of a new drug, sulphasuxidine, and that almost immediately checked Joy's dysentery and brought her temperature down to normal. Within days she had recovered.

From her point of view it was little short of a miracle, and since a letter was awaiting her telling that the staff in Los Angeles had met for a special period of prayer about her health, she knew why she had felt so unusually impelled to go on to Abra. They were linked together in a spiritual conflict, and their prayers for each other could turn the tide.

'Never fear about mentioning problems,' she wrote in answer to a letter from Virginia Miller, who told of acute and embarrassing financial shortage at Witmer Street. 'We love to take hold in prayer.

'As to why this has come, there are many obvious reasons for counterattack. One is the step of faith regarding making gramophones available below bottom production costs; another is the large output of records to the factory and the release of men to help us; the prospect of buying another press; and also the blitzkrieg that has been coming upon Mountain Province with the acquisition of these languages and dialects! My illness is doubtless connected with this same strategy, and this makes it a privilege.'

Then she went on,

'All the depressions and slim months in the world could not keep the Lord from sending us the money we need. He is supplying it. He cannot do otherwise. What God is doing is giving us a chance to suffer and believe so that He can work out a more precious and eternal weight of glory. A test isn't a test unless it is a *test!*

'We surely are standing by you all, and especially you, Virginia. God is doing marvels for us all. "Fear not, only believe." This trial is more precious to God because you are standing firm and trusting.'

A few weeks later she received a reply to this letter. Sufficient money had come in to pay all the bills, and business was proceeding as usual.

6

Angel Guides

'JUST CALL ME "Bring-'em-back-alive Sherwood" – that's my
name,' whispered Ann breathlessly. She was so excited she
could scarcely speak. She must tell Joy the whole story of what
had led up to obtaining the recordings they had been warned
they could never expect to get. It was past midnight, but she
couldn't sleep anyhow, nor Joy either, and lying in their
narrow camp beds in the Filipino house she described how she
had captured that Negrito.

They had heard about the Negritos and read about them
while they were in Manila. The little dark-brown aborigines,
timid and fleet as deer, living in the forest and off the forest,
moved about from one site to another like gypsies, and were
rarely seen anywhere else. Ever since they had arrived in the
northernmost tip of Luzon they had been asking the question,
'Do you see any Negritos here?' The response had always
been the same – a shake of the head and the words, 'No, not
here.' According to the anthropologist's report this was the
area where they were to be found, but until the two recordists
stayed in the home of the Spottswoods they met no-one who
could give them any information about the Negritos.

Mr. Spottswood, however, had actually found where some
of them lived. To do so had involved him in perilous trips in a
small private plane over six thousand feet mountains. The
great-hearted missionaries were planning to start a medical
work amongst them, and the prospect of taking in gramophones with Negrito recordings aroused a hope that died

almost as soon as it was born. It would be wonderful to be able
to pass on the Good News in their own tongue along with the
medicine! But how could these enthusiastic American women
with their heavy recording equipment reach the elusive forest-
dwellers, find someone who knew their language well enough
to communicate with them, and get recordings made in time to
be back in Manila on schedule for their next trip? Humanly
speaking, it was impossible. With other tribal groups, yes. In
most cases they could be contacted. But the Negrito aborigines
– only God could organise that.

'Oh, God – organise it for us . . . !'

Joy and Ann had moved on down the valley to a town
where Mrs. Maggay, a well educated Filipina Christian, had
agreed to record in the Ibanog language. They were in her
home right now, excitedly recounting in low murmurs the
events of the day. For that very afternoon, in this very room, a
teen-age Negrito had sat speaking into the microphone, his
ginger corkscrew hair quivering with amazement at the most
extraordinary thing that had ever happened in his life. For
when what he had said was played back, he heard a Negrito
voice – (it couldn't be his own!) speaking to him out of that
box.

It was too much for him. In a convulsion of laughter,
wonder, fear, a confusion of emotions too overwhelming to be
contained with dignity, he jerked over backwards, his whole
four foot of body involved in the only expression adequate to
the marvel.

It had gone on like this the whole afternoon and well on into
the evening – Ann crouching over the recorder, Joy speaking
in English, their Filipina hostess translating into Ibanog, a
toothless but agile little man translating it into Negrito, and the
Negrito himself speaking it in his own way. Every time what
he had said was played back to him the same thing had
happened. He jerked over backwards and shook with laughter.
But in spite of the regular delays, they were able to make
several recordings before he departed. They could still scarcely
believe it.

'How did you get him?' whispered Joy. It was the first time

they had had the opportunity to talk together, and Ann eagerly told her story.

It had all started with a disappointment, as Joy knew. They had had a lot of trouble with the recorder, but just after midday it had started working satisfactorily and they were ready to begin recording. Then, to their consternation, Mrs. Maggay had announced in her clear, careful English,

'An emergency has come about and I must go across town to do an errand.'

The deeply engrained attitude that all things work together for good stood up to the test. They did not display their inward alarm lest the generator wouldn't last out, and Ann cheerfully suggested that she should take Mrs. Maggay in the car, to save time. Mrs. Maggay had a friend who wanted a lift, too, and the three of them set out. It was on the way back that Ann had asked if any Negritos ever came here.

Yes, they came to town sometimes, she was told. They walked the five days from their camp once or twice a month. In fact, they had been in last Sunday, but had all gone away now . . .

Then Mrs. Maggay's friend said something to her in Ibanog, and Mrs. Maggay nodded.

'Oh, yes, he might know . . . Miss Sherwood, please stop right here!' Ann drew up sharply by the kerb, where an old man was sitting on a chair outside his shop. He had no teeth, but he was agile enough and smiling. After a few words with Mrs. Maggay he disappeared.

'In not more than two shakes of a lamb's tail he was back!' whispered Ann. 'And with him the Negrito!' A real live Negrito, clad in only a red loin cloth and his own brown velvet skin! 'Then Mrs. Maggay explained that Mr. Gonzales, the old man, could speak Negrito! Think of it! And he'd be glad to come to her house to help translate for our recordings!

'So that's how it happened. I poked around in the back of the car to make room for our little Negrito and he got in, bending over so he could stand without hitting his head. Then I let the seat back gently, to make sure it didn't crush him. It didn't so we moved over and made room for Mr. Gonzales to sit with us on the front seat. I was going to get them all back to the house or bust! "Bring-'em-back-alive Sherwood" – that's me!'

It was the highlight of those first months in the Philippines. They were on their way back to Manila by this time, travelling through the world-famous rice terraces of Bontoc, over the dangerous trail to Lubuagan. They recorded fifteen tribal languages there, with the help of Christian students in a Bible School. Arriving in Baguio they learned that a rumour had spread around that they were missing, possibly captured by Huk guerillas. The welcome they received was all the warmer because of the relief that was felt at seeing them. When at last they reached Manila and the shelter of the F.E.B.C./F.E.B.I.A.S. estate they had obtained recordings in forty languages and dialects.

'It is wonderful to be on the last lap of the work here,' wrote Joy to the team in Los Angeles, as she looked back over the Luzon trip. 'Each experience, though hard at the time, turns out to be so happy and delightful that it doesn't leave us always looking forward to something nicer – except, of course, home! That never fails to have a wooing charm. That almost seems too wonderful to be true, that we'll be there with all of you again! What an incentive!'

But there were eight more months to go, and the islands of Mindanao, Mindoro and Palawan to visit. They turned their attention to the next trip.

* * *

'Not go to Mindanao now? Wait until the autumn?'

Joy and Ann looked at each other in dismay, then again at the letter that had just arrived. It re-affirmed a warm welcome to Mindanao, but implied clearly that it would be wiser to postpone their visit until later in the year. They suddenly found themselves facing the thing they had dreaded.

'That means we'll have to go to Mindoro instead.'

'Mindoro! Now? Oh, no!'

Mindanao had seemed so safe and secure, with the

assurance of Christian and Missionary Alliance workers to meet them, arrange their itineraries, welcome them into their homes. The hardships in travel, the long hours crouching over the recorder, ears attuned to every sound, the inevitable bouts of dysentery, would all be alleviated by the ready help of the missionaries.

But on the island of Mindoro there were no missionaries. Around the coast the Filipinos in the towns and villages, as elsewhere in the Philippines, were Roman Catholic. Although it was said there were a few isolated Protestants here and there, no-one could provide the name of even one person who would be willing to help two American recordists to reach the Mangyan, the pagan tribes hidden away in the vast, steamy, jungle-clad mountains of the interior. Not surprisingly, therefore, Joy had decided first to visit the islands where there were missionaries, and having gained experience, finally to go to Mindoro.

This last minute reversal of plans, however, left them with no alternative if they were to accomplish what they had set out to do. They must go to Mindoro now, if they were to go at all, and they knew enough about travelling in the Philippines to shrink from the prospect. It would have been difficult enough if they could have gone by car, all their baggage piled up behind them, but there was no thought of taking a car to Mindoro. They would have to travel by bus down to the port of Batangas, taking their baggage with them, then get on a steamer taking their baggage with them, and when they arrived they would disembark and find themselves on the beach, their baggage with them . . . And then?

Where would they go with their baggage? How would they find the Mangyan, the tribal people hidden in the mountains? And even if they found them, how would they communicate without a bi-lingual middleman?

On the face of it, it was foolhardy to set out in such a fashion, on such an enterprise. They dared not do it, they agreed, unless they were absolutely sure they were in the Lord's plan. Joy, usually so energetic, now refused to be hurried. She refused to spend a lot of time studying the map of

Mindoro, either. What was the use of knowing the names of
the towns and villages round the coast, tracing the rivers that
flowed down through the jungles, guessing at where there
might be settlements of Mangyan up there in the impenetrable
mountains? What they needed was not a map, but a guide.

For some days she spent most of her time sitting reading
her Bible, chapter after chapter, praying and reading, praying
and reading, until her mind was saturated with the words and
certain phrases came to life, like little springs bubbling up from
the moist ground.

'And he brought forth his people with joy and his chosen
with gladness; and gave them the lands of the heathen.' Ps.
105:43,44. She was conscious of a quickening, but the authori-
tative word had not yet come. Then one day, reading in
Exodus, she came to Chapter 23:20.

'Behold, I send an angel before thee, to keep thee in the way,
and to bring thee into the place which I have prepared.'

That was it. An angel guide! What form the angel would
take she did not know. Perhaps someone with an aeroplane
that would turn up at the last minute, as happened once in
Alaska, and sweep them off, baggage and all, to their destination! Anyhow, the way was clear – they must prepare to go to
Mindoro, since God had assured them He would see them to
the place He had prepared for them.

Now it was all activity. Ann's hands were already full,
editing the tapes they were to send back to Los Angeles, so Joy
set about making the preparations for a journey that would be
different from anything they'd undertaken before.

No heavy trunks this time. All must be hand luggage they
could carry themselves. Cheap canvas bags, light rattan
suitcases, bedrolls and mosquito nets.

Rubber boots for walking through swamps.

Shoes with leather soles, since crepe soles melted in the heat.

Seersucker blouses and nylon skirts for easy washing.

Raincoats – it rained a lot in Mindoro.

Sweaters – it could be very cold in an open boat.

Medicines. They must be prepared for dysentery, malaria . . .

In addition to all that there was the heavy but indispensable electrical tape recorder requiring generator, electric cords, transformer, booster, volt meter and extra gasoline.

That recording equipment, weighing one hundred and fifty pounds, was the main problem, yet without it the whole trip would be pointless. Oh, for the protection of their own vehicle in which to store it, as on former occasions. How could the two of them, among strangers, keep their eyes on everything at once? How could they preserve it from getting damp or damaged – or stolen when they weren't looking? The obvious possibilities had to be faced and guarded against as much as possible – but not much was possible.

Then one day a parcel arrived from the U.S.A. addressed to Miss Joy Ridderhof. It was not very large, and when they unpacked it they saw a box of six by six by sixteen inches, covered with bright red imitation leather. A present from Al Rethey and Herman Dyk – they'd made it themselves, and hoped it would prove useful.

Joy and Ann gasped. It looked like a toy. It couldn't be a real tape recorder that worked on batteries.

But it was. Holding their breath they plugged in the microphone and made a trial recording, then played it back. Perfect! They tried again. Perfect! They examined it upside down and down side up, exclaiming with amazement when they realised that the batteries inside would last for a month, and that a spare set would be so small it could be slipped into a handbag.

It was unique. There was not another like it in all the world. No need now for the generator and the electric cords, the transformer and the booster, the volt meter and the extra gasoline and the heavy electrical tape recorder. Instead, just this one item that could be carried under the arm!

As things turned out, they could not have managed without it. Even at that point, its arrival transformed the situation for them, reducing their baggage so drastically. All the same, on the day when at last they boarded a crowded bus they waved a very reluctant goodbye to the group of F.E.B.C. friends who had come to see them off. They were embarking on the most hazardous journey they had ever undertaken. They did not

know where they would spend the night, they and their
baggage, how they would find their way to the steamer, what
they would do when they landed in Mindoro. It was like
stepping off the edge of a cliff into a void.

At this point God's secret service came into operation, as
they were passed from one unknown person to another until
they reached the Mangyan.

It started on the bus going to Batangas. 'Where you stay
in Batangas?' enquired the friendly Filipino conductor. Joy
didn't know, so rather lamely asked if he could recommend a
hotel. A whispered conversation, then his wife said shyly,
'We poor. Our house very small. We like you come to our
house?'

Joy beamed. Her excitement got the better of her theology
as she called out in Spanish to Ann, sitting farther back, 'Ann
– I've met an angel and his wife!' Then she said to the little
woman sitting beside her, 'We like very much come to your
house.'

Duly deposited with their baggage at the conductor's house,
there were various friends and relations to meet. Among them
was Caridad. 'My cousin. She live in Mindoro. She go to
Mindoro tomorrow. You like she go with you?'

'Oh, yes!' The exquisite wonder of it! *Behold, I send an
angel before thee to keep thee in the way* . . . 'Oh, yes! We like
very much Caridad go with us.'

The next morning they boarded the steamer for Mindoro,
Caridad in charge.

'Where you go in Mindoro?' asked Caridad conversation-
ally. They didn't know, but feeling they ought to say something replied rather uncertainly, 'We go Calahan.' They'd seen
the name on the map.

'Why you not go Nauhan?' she enquired.

Why not, indeed? One place is as good as another when you
know nothing about either.

'All right. We go Nauhan.'

They arrived in Mindoro, and Caridad saw the baggage was
all stowed on the little bus which they also boarded. They
bounced along the road through coconut groves and palm

trees until they came to Nauhan. God's secret service was operating flawlessly, although Caridad knew nothing about it. She just knew that these two American women were Protestants, and that her neighbours, Mr. and Mrs. Elpidio Adalia were Protestants also. She led Joy and Ann through a little gate, along a path to a wooden house and introduced them. She felt sure it would be a good place for them to stay.

It proved to be, indeed, the place that God had prepared for them. Mr. Adalia, home from Manila on a short vacation, was training for the Presbyterian ministry and welcomed them into his home. It became their Mindoro headquarters, from where they were put on the track of other isolated Protestant Filipinos who were able to lead them to the Mangyan.

The first were the Sulits of Bongabong. When Mr. and Mrs. Sulit got over their surprise at having two American women arrive at the foot of the ladder leading up to their *nipa* home they welcomed them with warm Filipino hospitality, but shook their heads when they were asked about Mangyan.

'We are so sorry. We rarely see any Mangyan. They are afraid of village people and now that it is the rainy season they don't come down from the hills.'

Joy and Ann were undaunted. 'We've asked God to send them to us,' they said, 'And we believe He will. Please look out for them,' and nine little Sulits spread eagerly around, watching for Mangyan, while Ann set up the tape recorder. An hour later the electrifying cry went out.

'Mangyans! Mangyans!' Sure enough, there they were — two teen-age boys with timid expressions on their bloated faces, long black hair tied back with string, emaciated bodies clad with loin cloths and not much else. They were selling wild orchids so that they could buy lime for the betel nut their people up in the hills were wanting.

'And one of them can speak Tagalog!' exclaimed Mr. Sulit, who had approached them gently so as not to frighten them away. 'That's why he's been sent to do the trading.'

The rest of the day and half of the next was spent squatting on the floor with the Sulits and the Mangyan, slowly, carefully speaking a sentence at a time in English — Tagalog —

Mangyan. Then the machine went into action, and the Mangyan sentence was captured and played back.

The reaction of the Mangyan was different from that of the Negrito as they listened to a Mangyan voice speaking out of the little red box. They were bewildered, breathless, rather apprehensive. But after a time they gained courage, the puckered brows smoothed, and they smiled. Before they left, four recordings had been made, and Joy and Ann moved on, too. There were other voices in Mindoro to capture.

When they left the island a month later they had obtained recordings in the tribal languages of five of the ethnic groups of the primitive, half-naked peoples of the inland mountains. Within a few months those people would be able to hear a box talking, telling in their own tongue, spoken by one of themselves, the amazing news that

> *Chief of Sky, He who made sky and earth and all in it, He send already message to all people of world. Message this in bundle of leaves they call 'Bundle of leaves what Chief of Sky says', and it tells how Chief of Sky give Son His, He has only one son, come to earth receive punishment of sins ours. He love us very much until He die on tree tied crosswise so that we not receive punishment in wicked village down below, place of fire and torment forever . . .*

It was July by this time, and in a little over four months their visas would expire. They returned to Manila and remained just long enough to edit the tapes and dispatch them to Los Angeles, write innumerable letters, then prepare for their next trips, to Palawan and finally to Mindanao. Then they set off again.

'It's the rainy season in Palawan,' they were warned. 'Torrential rains there. Most of the travelling has to be done by boat, too. Often held up by storms.'

They found it to be true as soon as they arrived. The home of the Filipino pastor who had invited them to stay was a cottage built out from the shore with the water lapping under it at high tide. For the first three days the rain beat down on the roof, drove across the sea obscuring the view, hemming them in.

'If it weren't so stormy I could take you over there tomorrow,' their host said, looking towards Culion. It was on this island, in 1906, that General Gordon had established what was for nearly half a century the biggest leprosy colony in the world. 'There's a man there who speaks Calamiano, and you could start recording. But we haven't seen the sun for weeks,' he continued with a sigh, 'And we couldn't go in rain like this.'

'Mr. Sosa,' said Joy earnestly. 'If you can furnish the boat and take us, I'm sure God will arrange the weather. He always does.' Then, sensing rather than seeing the amused glances that passed between some of the others in the room, she felt challenged. She knew God was able to still the incessant downpour, and she wanted Him to prove it. 'Let us pray now, ask Him to do it,' she said, and then and there closing her eyes, prayed aloud that all might hear.

The memory of that prayer was her first waking thought next morning, and she crept past Ann's recumbent form to go and peep out through the shutters. Was the sky clear? The massed bank of grey clouds, and the rush of rain on her face was the answer that drove her back into the room, and to her knees. It was not only that others might know that the Lord of whom she spoke was alive, ready to hear and answer prayer, but because there was so little time left for her and Ann to fulfil their task. Mr. Sosa, fisherman as well as pastor, would soon be too busy to spend his days with them. If they could not start on recording trips to neighbouring islands soon, it would be too late. *Lord, I praise You for what You're going to do!*

By nine o'clock that morning the rain had ceased. The fishing boat was launched, and they moved off . . .

*   *   *

Their journeys in the next few weeks took them from the northern tip of the Palawan group of islands to Brookes Point in the far south. It was here they encountered their deepest disappointment. For the first time in their trip to the Philippines they had to leave without making any recordings.

It was all the more humiliating because this particular

fortnight had been planned with such joyful enthusiasm and meticulous care by Sandy Sutherland and his wife. Months before, when these Brethren missionaries from Scotland heard about Gospel Recordings they had written urging Joy to come. 'Welcome Stop Large Opportunity for Records Here Stop' had been their telegraphed response to her preliminary letter, and they had spent hours preparing for the visit. Joy and Ann were welcomed with heart-warming eagerness.

'When at last we heard the guid news that you were coming to Palawan,' said Sandy in the deep Scottish brogue that years in the east had not dulled, 'often groups of us would sit together on the beach in the evenings and talk about it, wondering how soon we could expect you.' His wife had even translated some songs, with the help of an interpreter, into tribal languages, for it was known the records contained music. 'We have been practising with a selected quartette of guid voices, to be prepared for you.' Everything was ready, the little chapel was crowded, the bi-lingual Palawano was working on the scripts, the quartette was waiting to sing what they had been practising as Joy walked with Sandy towards the chapel. Passing the little houses on stilts that lay among the ferns and rich foliage of that quiet, palmy Eden, her excitement was intense. They had had a trying time at their previous port of call, with the recorder going out of action for days until, almost at the last moment, in answer to urgent prayer, Ann had discovered the fault, and all had gone well again. It had been a spiritual conflict, but although they had almost given up, they'd won through in the end. It had left them somewhat exhausted, however, and it was a relief to know that the recorder was working properly now. With so much preparation and prayer, this trip to Brookes Point promised to be one of the most profitable and pleasurable yet.

Then, as they entered the chapel, Joy's heart sank. Ann was crouching over the machine, and she was pulling it to pieces. Something had gone wrong again, and there were no technicians to help here.

'We usually have a test like this to begin with,' Joy told the Sutherlands. It was no unusual experience, and they could understand that. 'But it always works eventually so that we get the records. Let's just keep on rejoicing!'

But this time it was different. They prayed, they praised, they spent hours working on the recorder, trying everything they could think of, but the result was always the same. No response. The machine was dead. It remained the same for the two weeks they were at Brookes Point.

'Said I not unto thee, if thou wouldest believe thou shouldest see the glory of God?' was the text Joy spoke on, the last Sunday they were there. It was the word Jesus had spoken to Martha at the grave of her brother, when all human hope had died. It seemed appropriate to the occasion, and as she spoke Joy glowed with faith. But the next day, aboard the little inter-island steamer that was to carry them north again, she wrote rather wearily in her diary, 'Monday, August 21. Left Brookes Point without any recordings.' Then she added valiantly, 'The Lord teaches our hands to war. We are learning more about spiritual warfare, and have many opportunities to rejoice.'

Elsewhere in her little notebook she had written something else. The words were simply, 'Lastani – Farm School, Aborlan'. It was the name and address of a Palawano boy from Brookes Point who was bi-lingual. She'd made a note of it, just in case ... And also that there were three girls from Brookes Point at school in Puerto Princesa, farther up the coast, who had learned some of the songs that had been translated. She'd made a note of that, just in case ... One must keep on the alert, for one never knew what God might be preparing. One didn't rejoice for nothing.

It was on that boat moving away from Brookes Point, the place of such perplexing disappointment, that light began to dawn. Before the day was out Joy had added to that morning entry, 'A friend from Aborlan is on our boat. He is a judge there, and assures us that he will go to the Farm School to request that Lastani be allowed to go to Puerto Princesa to help us for a few days!'

The next day there was a single entry, 'Arrived in Puerto Princesa Tuesday evening.'

Wednesday's entry read, 'The recorder has been at the shop all day. The trouble seems to be a broken wire which goes into the plug of one of the B. batteries.'

Thursday's entry, 'Lastani is here! He is translating the scripts one after another, writing them beautifully, reading them with fluency and such expression. The recorder is working off and on. But gradually we are getting the records.'

Over the weekend the three schoolgirls were located and brought along. Yes, they remembered the songs they had learned. They sang them clearly and sweetly.

So the Palawano recordings were made after all.

Joy never sent a more jubilant, praiseful telegram to anyone than that which was dispatched to the Sutherlands at Brookes Point. The whole experience had tested her faith to an unusual degree. She had sensed the deep disappointment of the missionaries who had worked and prayed so much in antici-pation of the visit which was to provide them with the wonderful new means of spreading the Gospel in the languages they themselves could not speak. It had been contrary to all her former experience to continue day after day, right to the very end of the arranged fortnight, believing and rejoicing in expectation of a sudden solution that this time was not given. 'It *always* works eventually so that we get the records,' she had asserted on that first evening, and she had fully expected that before the end of the visit it would happen. It would be such an encouragement to the young believers whom the missionaries had been preparing so enthusiastically – strengthen their faith! Surely God would do it!

But God's ways *are* past finding out. He who had stilled the storm in response to her cry in the fisherman's cottage delayed His answer at Brookes Point. The satisfaction of achievement was known elsewhere than at the place and with the people she most desired to enjoy it. She was learning that He works to no set pattern.

The last two months of the Philippines trip were in some ways the easiest of all. Down in the southern island of Mindanao missionaries had prepared itineraries for the recordists, and interpreters and transport were provided too.

Joy and Ann had to spend more time than usual in writing new scripts to make their message relevant to ethnic groups whose culture and beliefs were different from those in the islands farther north, but long hours of work were less strain than the spiritual conflicts they had encountered earlier.

'We see the Lord's hand upon us for good in so many ways, I never can fathom His tenderness and thoughtfulness,' wrote Joy gratefully in her diary during those months. She saw in the smoothing of the pathway evidence of her Master's care that others often failed to observe. 'He is so unpretentious about what He does. You have to be wide awake to observe all the intricate design in it.'

Even on the occasion when they launched out on their own in response to the unexpected approaches of a loud-voiced young woman who undertook to 'find you languages' they ended up in surroundings so delectable they felt they had been to a luxury home on Hollywood hills. The loud-voiced young woman who appeared from nowhere as they sat in a hot little restaurant waiting to cross a ferry, told them she worked at a gold mine, and that there she would find them some languages. Stranger as she was, she displayed some of the characteristics that Joy had loved in the bold, fearless Cruzita of Marcala. Joy was prepared to trust her, even though the story of the gold mine sounded rather far-fetched. The promise of more languages could not be ignored. So they went with her, and sure enough, her story proved to be true. There was a gold mine, and there were people connected with it who spoke two of the languages they wanted to capture. The most fantastic part of the whole escapade, however, was that their guide had entry to the luxurious cottage on the hills above the mine, which was used by the director when he visited the place. A relative of hers was the resident cook. So for two days Joy and Ann enjoyed baths and showers in a tiled bathroom with running water, beds with interior-spring mattresses, iced drinks and good American food, perfectly cooked and served. After the steamy plains where their bodies were always sticky and the beds hard, it was like entering a dream-world. But the crowning triumph of the whole adventure was to obtain recordings in the language of the fierce and practically inaccessible Manobo tribe. The smiling cook in the dream-world happened to be a Manobo, and was only too happy to oblige!

When eventually they boarded the United States freighter that was to take them back across the Pacific they had obtained recordings in ninety-two languages. In half of them no part of the Bible had been translated, nor was the Gospel known. So ended for them the most momentous and significant year of their lives.

7

What is a Leader?

WHAT IS A LEADER? The question has been the subject of innumerable debates and evoked various definitions. Indispensable qualities have been enumerated and characteristics analysed, and the probability is that Joy Ridderhof would have been considered to lack too many of them to lay claim to the title. Certainly she would have said so, had she stopped to think about it.

'Joy never saw herself as being anyone important,' her secretary said of her years after she was acknowledged as the Founder-Director of an organisation of worldwide significance. 'If I want to talk to her about something I don't have to go to her — I just ask her if she'll come along to my office and see me, and she comes! What other boss would act that way?'

If, however, a leader is simply someone going ahead whom others are following, as the word suggests, then she was a leader. She did not go ahead alone, although she was prepared to do so. In fact, she was so set on achieving her goal that she scarcely stopped to look round, figuratively speaking, to see if anyone was following or not! But others were following. They were those who had been stirred to action by her single-mindedness and enthusiasm, and there was also that about her which commanded their loyalty and devotion. She knew and loved them all, keeping in touch with them individually even when she was away. She was a prolific writer of letters and short scribbled notes, which she sent off to all sorts of people, especially those connected with her in her all-absorbing work.*

'My soul is fired more and more with the desire to reach the uttermost part of the globe with the simple, clear story of salvation,' she had written two years before going to the Philippines, and the desire had become a consuming passion after the year spent there. She had seen for herself some of the little tribes of whose very existence she had been ignorant, and realised they were representative of far larger numbers in other countries. The Wycliffe Bible Translators who had first assessed them at about 2,000 were already raising the figure as surveys brought more of them to light. The vast unexplored forests of South America, the mountains of south-east Asia, the luxuriant jungles of Indonesia and New Guinea, the grasslands and deserts and forests of Africa – little pockets of humanity were hidden away in all of them. It would take decades to evangelise them by usual missionary methods, but with the unique techniques developed by Gospel Recordings the situation could be transformed.

She and Ann had talked about the possibilities while they were in the Philippines. If two middle-aged women with no experience of the Far East could obtain 92 languages in a year, what could not be done by teams of young men ready to venture for Christ with the same dedication so many of them had shown when battling for liberty during the years of the Second World War? Superficial as the method might seem, providing a gramophone and a few records that ran for three and a half minutes into which the basic truths of the Gospel had been compressed, there was overwhelming evidence that it was effective. Letters were coming in to the office in Witmer Street weekly, sometimes daily, telling of the amazing response as people in Africa, South America, Alaska and now the Philippines, listened to the voice of one of their own speaking in the language they could understand.

Mountains Singing by Sanna Morrison Barlow, the story of the Philippines trip, was compiled almost entirely from the reports Joy sent back, produced on the spot as she and Ann Sherwood moved from one place to another in the archipelago.

'Thank you for the records. It gives us a good feeling down inside our hearts every time we place another one. They play away in saloons where I myself don't enjoy going. When an illiterate buys a Gospel of Mark the tug on my heart is one of pain rather than joy ... "Will he find someone to read it to him?" But when an illiterate gets a record, he and dozens of other illiterates can all listen.'

'A good-natured old lady shop-keeper had an electric pick-up and I asked her if she would like to play some of my Hindi records. She consented, but listened with the usual guarded indifference of these Mohammedan people. However, others gathered to listen ... and drew the attention of a blind beggar going by with his dog leading him. He became so interested that the old lady bought the two records to keep and play them for the sake of the blind beggar.'

'A South American Indian ... acquired a gramophone and a record set and proceeded on a journey to a remote section of his tribe. Once again the voice in the little box told its story, in still another language, and five families believed. They systematically carried the gramophone from hut to hut urging their neighbours to believe and become as happy as they ...'

'I am keeping a rough note of the approximate number of Buhid Mangyan who have heard the records. To date over 150, and six Bangon who also understood ...'

'I have just returned from a trek into an area ... here in the Sudan. There has never been a ministry in this area before. I wish you could have seen some of these meetings as they listened to the eight records which we had. They were played over and over and over, and the songs learned. Since this is a minority group whose language we do not speak, these records are virtually in themselves building up these believers. Now that we have this wonderful new selection we can hardly wait to get back amongst them ...'

'The first set of records sent to an Eskimo group in November was so popular that it was almost worn out by Christmas. From early morning until late at night the people played them. The children memorised the Scripture they heard so often and happily quoted it the live-long day.'

'By way of these records you are able to send out missionaries that are able to talk but do not need to sleep nor eat!'

So it went on. The steady inflow of such letters and the
increasing demand for the records were an encouragement, but
also a challenge to faith. There were enough orders to keep the
team fully occupied and working overtime, but was that a
reason to refrain from obtaining more languages? Was it not
rather an incentive to press on, and to pray that God would
bring more technicians for the factory, more workers for the
despatch department, more secretaries for the administration —
and above all, more recordists to go to the field? Joy and Ann
were ready to set out again, but if recordings were to be made
in every language and dialect, they could not do it alone.

More field recordists. It was the primary need, and perhaps
the most difficult one to meet. It required not only technical
skill and resourcefulness, but a strong constitution, ability to
adapt to extremes of both climate and living conditions, and a
faith in God sufficient for every emergency and uncertainty.

'Simultaneous recording in various countries,' said Joy.
'That is the way to do it. And it's a job that in many cases can
only be undertaken by men.'

She was in great demand as a speaker, not only at public
meetings, but also in colleges and Bible seminaries, and
responded readily to invitations to tell what was being accomplished through Gospel Recordings, and what remained to be
done. Her speaking itineraries took her far and wide in the
U.S.A., then over the border into Canada, to the Prairie Bible
Institute in Alberta. One of their graduates, whom Joy met
later, was Vaughn Collins, in his early twenties. He was not
only willing to respond to the challenging call that came to him
as he listened to Joy's message, but he was also ready. The
Prairie Bible Institute required a very high degree of
renunciation on the part of its students. Discipleship to Jesus
Christ demanded that His work must come before everything
else, even the satisfaction of legitimate personal desires in the
choice of a career or a partner in marriage. The young
American, tall, lean, self-disciplined, had already settled these
matters in his own heart, and his years in forestry service

before entering the Bible Institute had nerved him for hardship and strenuous effort. He applied to Gospel Recordings, and was accepted.

A few months later another young student from the Prairie Bible Institute arrived at Joy's office in Los Angeles. Don Richter of the U.S. Marines had fought in the battle of Okinawa in the Second World War, and it was in the midst of that grim conflict he had made up his mind life was too uncertain to be spent doing anything short of the will of God. What it might be for him he did not know, but a conversation with Vaughn Collins eventually brought him to Gospel Recordings headquarters to apply to become a field recordist. As he listened to Joy telling him of the thrilling prospect of completing the task of getting the Gospel message 'to every creature' in our own generation by means of the recording techniques God had given them, he was inspired afresh, ready to set off on the next boat. He was scarcely prepared, therefore, for her reaction to his offer.

'Don,' she said, 'If you come to Gospel Recordings we don't promise to send you off on field work. You come to join a team, and you must be willing to do anything. Most of our workers stay around here doing mundane jobs — working in the factory, doing carpentry repairs, shipping out boxes of records, building little gramophones. It's all absolutely essential to the job of sending out the Gospel, and it's just as much a work of faith as going to the field. Are you willing for that?'

It was a sobering prospect, as Joy knew it would be, but she knew she must be honest. Plans were already afoot for her to go off on another recording trip, accompanied by Ann, Sanna Barlow and Vaughn Collins. If Don were to go to the field work abroad, it could not be now, and meanwhile, was he willing for this test? He had known the heat of battle and taken his directions from stern-faced men. He had been ready for anything on the beaches under gunfire — was he ready for anything now, even working in a little factory in down-town Los Angeles with an organisation directed by a woman? Only the assurance that it was the will of God would bring him to that point, and she waited for his answer.

She was not worried about it. It was not her responsibility. If God wanted Don Richter in Gospel Recordings He would make it plain, and He'd work out all the details. He always did.

Don Richter accepted the conditions. This was the way God was leading him, and he was prepared to follow. He came to join the team of workers in Witmer Street in June, 1952, without any assurance that he would ever be appointed to field recording.

Meanwhile, the plans for the recordist team of four to proceed together to Indonesia had gone awry. Vaughn had come in for some teasing about the project, and been asked laughingly, 'What are you going to do with these three women?' to which he had retorted, 'Oh, I'll just walk ahead and leave them to carry my luggage along after me!' But in the event, he had to go alone. They had booked four berths on a liner bound for Singapore, but a few days before they were due to leave, all their luggage packed and ready for bonding, they learned that there was only one berth available. They had omitted to make a down payment, so the other three berths had been taken. The omission had not been due to an oversight, merely to a lack of the money necessary at the time, and now it was too late.

Joy, as always, took an optimistic view of the situation. God must have a different plan for them, and He would lead them into it. It was as simple as that. Arrangements were altered, Vaughn set off across the Pacific on his own while Joy, Ann and Sanna, praising and praying together, looked out for another way of getting to the Far East. They would have to get to Singapore by a circuitous route instead of going there direct, Joy decided, and they would make some recordings on the way. She was already corresponding with Mr. Robert Short in Australia about the scattered tribes of aborigines there, so they would go that way. And that is how it came about that they arrived at the Mascot Airport, Sydney, on July 20, to be met by the local representative of the International Missionary Fellowship. His name was Stuart Mill.

They did not know at the time that his reception of the request to meet three American women had been unfavourably coloured by a previous experience when a similar request had landed him with an American woman who expected him to arrange meetings for her, spend hours on her arrangements, and generally act as her factotum. He was more than willing to help bona-fide missionaries on their way and frequently did so, but enthusiastic free-lances with novel ideas presented a different case. He had never heard of Miss Joy Ridderhof nor of Gospel Recordings. Evidently she was coming with two companions to do something about producing gramophone records, 'We've got plenty of them already,' he thought. Stuart Mill's Christian courtesy impelled him to meet the three strangers, but beyond that he could not commit himself. His wife was in hospital, and he had too much on his hands. He arrived at the air terminal with a utility van into which they helped him pile their thirty-four pieces of baggage, saw them comfortably settled inside, themselves, then took his place at the driver's seat.

Joy sat beside him. Wishing to show a reasonable interest in the visitors he enquired politely what they were hoping to do. He understood it had something to do with gramophone records?

It was the one conversational opening above all others to which Joy always responded with whole-hearted fervour. Yes, gramophone records — telling the Gospel in the languages of primitive tribes! The wonder of it never failed to thrill her and as they sped along the road towards the guest house where they were to spend the night Ann and Sanna exchanged amused glances. Joy could talk a streak when Gospel records were the subject! She referred to some of those they had produced already, explained the process by which they were obtained, the results they were bringing. She only stopped talking long enough for Stuart Mill to ask terse questions, then replying to them went on again. She was always glad to tell anyone what God was doing through Gospel Recordings.

When they arrived at their destination she and her two companions thanked Mr. Mill warmly for all the help he had given them. They were going on to Melbourne the next day to meet Mr. Short of the Unevangelised Fields Mission about getting recordings of aborigines in Australia and New Guinea, they told him. 'Thank you so much, Mr. Mill. Goodbye . . .'

So that was it. He had fulfilled his obligation to the Interdenominational Missionary Fellowship, and was committed to nothing more. But as he drove back to his home he suspected that the fifteen minutes' conversation in the van was to change the whole course of his life.

The Trio went on to Melbourne. There they learned more about the aborigines of Australia and the tribes of New Guinea. To obtain recordings of some of those peoples was something a woman could not attempt, they were told. Quite apart from the dangers and hardships, carriers and guides would only travel with a man, and without them no stranger could find the way. 'You must have a man to do that sort of work.'

Joy thought of Don Richter. The courage and the resourcefulness that would be required for the peculiarly hazardous task of reaching those out-of-the-way and in some cases fierce tribes were qualities that had already been developed in the ex-Marine. He had offered for field recording, and she knew it was what he wanted to do, or she might have hesitated to suggest an assignment so fraught with danger. But as it was, she had no doubt that he was the one for this job. She wrote back to Los Angeles, 'Tell Don we need him for the aborigine work in this country as soon as possible.'

When Don Richter received the message he only had $30 to his name, but he remembered something one of the Trio had said to him. 'Don't worry about finances. When the Lord's time comes, He will just thrust you out.' Whatever his feelings might be, he'd go ahead and make the necessary arrangements, and see what happened. Passport, visa, inoculations . . . Visits to boat companies to enquire about a passage to Sydney. Here he was brought to a halt. Ships were booked for as much as a couple of years ahead, he was told, with Australian war brides going home for a visit. But eventually he was offered a booking, with just one week in which to put down the first payment. On the morning of the day it was due he was still without the money, but by noon two gifts for him amounting to U.S. $200 had been received in the Gospel Recordings treasurer's office. One was from the Prairie Bible Institute.

He got to the shipping office in time to secure that passage. Less than two months after receiving Joy's message he arrived in Sydney, dressed ready to strike the trail . . .

But before that happened, Joy had met Stuart Mill again. With Ann and Sanna she had returned to Sydney, en route for New Guinea where arrangements were being made for them to get recordings from accessible tribes. On this occasion Stuart Mill not only met them, but took them to stay in his own home, and there they heard in detail his story.

He and his wife Molly had been missionaries in the Solomon Islands. They had returned to Australia for family reasons, and he had gone into business, but they had never relinquished the idea of some day going back. They had, indeed, taken steps to do so, but another family emergency had held them up, and by the time they were ready to go the special vacancy Stuart was prepared to fill had been occupied by someone else.

It was at this point he had met the Trio at the Mascot Airport. As soon as he heard Joy talk of gramophones playing records in tribal languages his mind had flashed back to the islands he knew so well. He thought of the many times he had watched the fuzzy-haired inhabitants crouching enthralled around wheezy gramophones that played jazz tunes and crooning love songs, listening to words they could not even understand. What would have happened if he could have changed those cracked old records for those that spoke and sang the Gospel in the tongue the listeners understood! He remembered the many little hamlets he had visited when cruising in the *Evangel* round the islands. He had preached in those hamlets once or twice, then had to move on. What would it have meant to be able to leave Gospel Records behind so that the message was repeated time and time again after he had gone? What could be accomplished if Gospel records in all the great variety of dialects in the Pacific islands could be distributed to them all?

Before he reached home that evening the seed thoughts of a

Gospel Recordings Branch in Australia had been sown in his mind. As he talked it over later with Molly the pattern clarified. On the top floor of his factory was a large empty space which could be used for storing records. He could undertake the distribution and promote the work. That was what he wanted to talk to Joy about when she returned from Melbourne.

'Why, that's just what we've been praying for,' was her excited response. 'The three of us saw the potential here in this country, and just prayed and prayed that the Lord would raise up someone to be responsible for distributing the records. And you want to do it! Now, isn't that wonderful!'

They went on to discuss the broad principles on which Gospel Recordings operated.

'Pray about everything — no public or private appeals for money. Look to God to supply your needs. Every worker in G.R. does that, knows personally the way of faith. Records all given away free. And rejoice!' Joy beamed as she proclaimed her favourite theme. 'God is Almighty. He makes everything work for His purpose, even when we make mistakes!'

Once Stuart Mill had an idea and an aim, he lost no time in unnecessary reflection. The thing to do was to publicise this new method of capturing voices to preach in languages not yet even translated. The people most likely to welcome it would be missionaries. They knew where there were unreached tribal groups in their own areas presenting a mute, unconscious appeal to which there was no way to respond. They would be the people to help in providing information and local interpreters. He therefore invited leaders of all the missionary societies he knew to come and meet Miss Joy Ridderhof of Gospel Recordings Inc., from America. That would get things started, and they could move on from there.

The outcome of that meeting was a visit from the director of a Christian radio fellowship. 'I have just this morning received a letter from one of our workers, David Hogan,' he told Joy. 'He has been in Borneo trying to get a permit to establish a Christian radio broadcast, but he finds it can't be obtained. He asked if I would be willing to loan him to Gospel Recordings.

Don't know how he heard about you, but there it is. Would it be possible for him to join you for a time?'

Joy thought immediately of Vaughn Collins. She had felt uneasy about him. They seemed to have left him stranded in Singapore, but she hadn't known what to do, except pray for the Lord to make His own way plain. Here was the answer.

'Why, it's just what we've been needing,' she said. 'Someone to team up with Vaughn. Vaughn could go with him to Borneo and make recordings there.' Gospel Recordings was really moving in the Southern Hemisphere! In Stuart Mill Joy had found someone as eager as she. As they looked into the future together, he said, 'If there's anything else I can do — any other way in which we can help.'

He can have had no idea how preposterous a suggestion would be put to him in response to that offer. Joy knew exactly what she wanted, and the fact that there was no known means by which it could be obtained did not disturb her at all. Her mind leapt straight to the end, and when she knew what it was, she prayed that the means would be provided. Now, with this quiet, efficient, experienced Australian engineer before her, she saw the possibility of the means being provided to obtain the end she had in mind.

'We need a gramophone without any mechanism that can go wrong,' she told him. 'Something that the most primitive people, something that even a child can use without breaking it. A hand-wind, motorless machine. Even with the very simple machines our factory in Los Angeles is turning out now, things go wrong with the mechanism from time to time. Then, of course, people can't listen to the records any more. They don't know how to mend the machines. Sometimes there are missionaries in the vicinity who can put things right, but not always. A hand-wind, motorless gramophone. That's what we need. If God would help you to invent that ... I've been praying about it for years,' she added.

Stuart looked at her. He knew far better than she what a well-nigh impossible thing she was asking. But he knew, as she knew, that without that simple hand-wind gramophone much of what was being attempted on behalf of the people in earth's remotest ends would fall far short of what could be accomplished. His mind, too, leapt to the desirable end; then, as it were, started working backwards to discover the means. Nothing was impossible – with God. God had helped these women to develop a technique whereby anyone in the world could, in a single interview, proclaim the simple message of salvation in his own tongue. God could help him, Stuart Mill, to invent something whereby anyone could go on hearing it!

She moved on soon after that. She had not come to Australia for the purpose of opening a new centre, or promoting the work of Gospel Recordings. She had crossed the Pacific to capture languages, to add more tongues and voices to the great multitude that should one day stand together praising Him who sits upon the throne of the universe. God had called Stuart Mill to start a Gospel Recordings centre in Australia, and God would show him how to do it. Now she must go on . . .

. . . to new Guinea, to capture some of those languages.

. . . to Singapore to meet Vaughn and give him the training he needed before he branched out as a recordist with David Hogan.

. . . back to Australia to help Don in the same way when he arrived. They must both be shown how to get the best out of their recording machines, how to splice the tapes accurately, cut out the stutters, erase clicks. How to keep accurate notes of everything. How to select from the many scripts she and Ann had produced those that would be most suitable for each different language group. Then they would be ready to launch out on their own, discover as she had discovered that 'He that followeth Me shall not walk in darkness, but shall have the light of life.' Young men, given in answer to prayer, going to do a man's work! Simultaneous recording teams, pressing forward.

For herself and Ann and Sanna, India lay waiting, and the surrounding countries. It was not without a sense of urgency that they had set out from Los Angeles, and it was not without a sense of urgency that they left Australia now. The open doors in China that had offered such promise at the conclusion of the Second World War had closed completely, cutting off one fifth of the human race. Other countries were threatened in Asia and Africa, and who could foretell how long the opportunities that existed at present for capturing the voices of earth's hidden people would last?

Joy moved on. Others were following. Don Richter hit the trail among the aborigines in Australia, Vaughn Collins and David Hogan in south-east Asia. Three or four workers had joined Gospel Recordings in Australia, making and sending out gramophones, installing equipment for pressing records, distributing those that came in bulk supplies from Los Angeles. And Stuart Mill, between taking trips to the Solomon Islands to capture voices, speaking at meetings, promoting the work, was applying his ingenious mind to the problem of inventing a motorless gramophone that a child could work, and that would not go wrong.

8

To Africa

JOY HAD NOT planned to return to Los Angeles in 1954, neither did she particularly want to go, although she reacted in the usual way. 'Rejoice! The Lord is going to work out something real good!' But the opportunities for obtaining recordings in the Far East had proved more numerous than she had expected. With Ann and Sanna she had travelled in Assam, where Ben Wati, first encountered when he was a student in Wheaton, introduced them to his own people of Nagaland; to Nepal, a closed land for centuries but now opening as the result of the overthrow of the influential Ranas; to Pakistan, Kashmir, Burma. And India. India had burdened her mind to an unusual degree, made her conscious not only of the little remote tribes that never failed to challenge her, but also of the surging masses of people whose poverty and illiteracy made their own piteous appeal. Here in India with its hundreds of millions of people, the most populous nation in the free world now that China had fallen to Communism, were countless multitudes who were accessible geographically, but hemmed in by the stranglehold of Hinduism and their own inability to read. The introduction into village homes or crowded city tenements of a little gramophone with records that proclaimed the Gospel of Jesus Christ in terms they could understand could be a means of reaching them that normal missionary methods and the distribution of tracts and books often failed to achieve. The opportunities for using the peculiar techniques God had enabled Gospel Recordings to develop were pressing in on her, and she knew much waited to be done in India, even though plans were already on foot for her to go with Ann and Sanna to Africa.

In the light of those opportunities, the administrative claims of the Headquarters of G.R. in Los Angeles seemed weak indeed, and she did not return of her own choice. But an urgent request had come, a crisis had developed in the work that could not be ignored. Joy was the Director, and she must leave the other two to fulfil the recording programmes arranged while she went back to deal with the sort of situation for which she felt little suited. Already it was becoming evident that she was a pioneer rather than an administrator.

As often happened, what appeared to be a hindrance in her activities eventually proved to be an extension of them. Her arrival in Los Angeles coincided with the visit there on business of an electronics consultant from England named Livingston Hogg. He had heard something about Gospel Recordings by way of a missionary in Iceland who told a friend of his of it, and since he was in the vicinity he decided to visit the headquarters of the little organisation. Joy, delighted at his interest, not only took him all over the factory and offices, but obligingly chauffeured him to some of the places he had to go to in the course of his business, offering to show him some of the sights into the bargain. The problem in the work that had brought her back demanded her decisions more than her time, and she always enjoyed driving around her own city and showing it off to visitors. As a guide, she was easily diverted. She usually became so absorbed in telling her passengers of the wonderful way in which God was opening things up for the Gospel records, the amazing stories of conversions that were constantly being received, the answers to prayer and the provisions God made, that she forgot all about the sights she had brought her friends to see. Time could always be profitably occupied when sitting in a car, she felt. On one occasion she took a party out to see the famous Millionaires' Mile in Hollywood, and on the way suggested that they should have a prayer meeting as they drove along. Prayer came to her as naturally as talking, and as they cruised along the broad boulevards she reminded the Lord of the recordists out on the field and their needs, the ill-health of this one, the family problems of that one, the particular piece of machinery they were needing in the factory . . . 'And we praise Thee, Lord, that Thou wilt work it all out . . .'

Her passengers closed their eyes and followed her prayer sincerely enough, but when it was finished one of them asked, 'Joy, when do we come to the Millionaires' Mile?' to which she answered with dismay, 'Oh! We've passed that long ago!'

What experiences Livingston Hogg may have had along this line he did not relate publicly, but he had evidently appreciated what she had done to make his visit enjoyable, and warmly invited her to stay with him and his wife when she came to England. He was very interested in her work, he intimated, and thought others would be, too. So some time later, on her way to re-join Ann and Sanna, now in Kenya, she unsuspectingly accepted the offer, little knowing what was in store for her. She arrived at the comfortable, spacious home of the Livingston Hoggs in Hampstead to learn that a reception had been arranged at which she was to be the guest of honour. It was to be held in a hotel in the West End, and a number of well-known Christian leaders had been invited to meet her. Representatives of the Christian press would also be present.

Joy was really alarmed. It sounded so very, very formal, so very, very English. To church banquets in her own country she was accustomed, but what might not be required of her at a reception in a hotel in London, England? That it was merely a buffet tea did little to allay her apprehensions, for how out of place could an American from Los Angeles be at a function so typically English. And what did one wear for a buffet tea?

A hat. She had a little black hat, suitable for almost any occasion, and thought that would be all right. Gloves, too, that went with it. But what about a suit, or a dress? Standing in her bedroom, she suddenly remembered the frock a friend in Chicago whom she had visited on her way over, had given to her. 'Whatever will I do with it?' she had thought at the time. 'It's too fancy. I shan't want to be dressed up in Africa. We'll be working there all the time!' But now, the frock came into its own. It was surely just the thing for an elegant, formal English reception and buffet tea in a hotel in the West End!

'So there we were, and I was the speaker,' she reported privately later, 'Little I! It wasn't big I, I can tell you that! I was really glad that I had the right clothes. I was really glad that friend in Chicago took the trouble to give it to me, when I had no idea how I would use it. So I think I was quite properly dressed. Oh yes, she gave me a brooch, too, and it was the kind that you'd need for England. It wasn't a gaudy one at all. It was made of silver, and had a stone in the middle of it. So I knew I was fixed up just right. So there I was, and the whole programme after they had the refreshments and went around one to the other was Joy Ridderhof. You can't imagine how scared I was! I didn't dream of any such thing.' However uneasy she may have felt at the outset, her fears vanished as she started on her favourite theme. The masculine faces, many of them emerging from clerical collars, quickened with interest or relaxed into smiles as she told her story, and the reporters' pencils flew across their notebooks. But for one, at least, of the invited guests, something more than interest was aroused.

Gilbert Vinden had gone to China in 1920, so when in 1950 the Communist Government made it impossible for missionaries to remain, he might have been considered due for retirement anyway. However, he did not take to the idea. 'I'm not ready for the shelf yet!' he said. There must be something he could still do to further the missionary cause. This new way of evangelising through gramophones and records captured his imagination immediately. If only he had had something like it in China! 'If there's any way in which my wife and I can help, we'll be ready,' he intimated after he had heard Joy speak. There was something to work on here! This was an organisation people ought to know about. And why not a distribution centre for records in England, where missionaries from Africa, Europe, the Near East, India, were constantly coming and going?

The seeds of the English branch of Gospel Recordings were sown at that buffet tea.

Meanwhile Joy went on to Africa to rejoin Ann and Sanna.

The three of them had lived together, travelled together, worked together, prayed together and faced emergencies together in such close proximity and in such a variety of situations that they fitted together like pieces of a jigsaw puzzle. Joy was the leader and shouldered the responsibility, making the arrangements, interviewing officials, dealing with the correspondence, keeping in touch with the work at Los Angeles, besides speaking frequently in church or chapel services. Ann, strongest of the three physically, cheerfully bore the burdens, crouching hour after hour over the tape recorder, patiently reading the scripts, waiting as each sentence passed through the interpreter, then indenting the right key of the tape recorder at the right moment to capture the tribal voice; editing and splicing the tapes when the recording process was over; going off to find a technician when the machine went wrong. Sanna the youngest, although unaccustomed by upbringing to roughing it, was game for every situation, doing the work of a recordist and watching all the time to see when she could quietly step in and give her aid in other ways. She had learned to recognise the danger signals that appeared when pain or weariness were taking their toll, especially of Joy. Joy was always likely to be beset by attacks of dysentery or malaria, legacy of the years in Marcala, but she insisted on ignoring them, making plans and taking journeys as though they did not exist until in the end they got the better of her.

'Joy just doesn't think of herself,' said Sanna. It was a simple statement of fact, and the fact faced her daily. Joy didn't consider herself when making her plans so she, Sanna, must do it for her, remembering what medicines might be needed, which clothes, secreting little items in the baggage to make food or drink more tasty, to be produced at appropriate moments to tempt jaded appetites.

So they travelled through Africa, the three of them, usually staying with missionaries, sometimes in such hotels as they could find, on occasions sleeping in the jeep. Sleeping in the jeep was somewhat precarious, as Joy discovered one night when the plank on which she was balancing slipped, and she found herself reclining at a most uncomfortable angle. However, she decided to stick it out rather than wake the others by moving. 'You were both fast asleep, and you needed to be,' she explained when they remonstrated on learning what had happened. 'You were tired out. I was, too,' she added with a grin, 'but it gave me some G.R.P.!' They knew what that meant. When things went well, Joy rejoiced. When they didn't go well, she asserted it was Good Rejoicing Practice. So whichever way things went, you rejoiced.

She had her greatest opportunity to rejoice in the face of difficulties, however, in connection with Ethiopia. Ethiopia, the country to which she had always been so drawn, to which in her youth she had been sure she would go, still drew her. 'We must go to Ethiopia,' she said eagerly, and wrote off to the missionaries in Addis Ababa hoping that arrangements could be made, as in other places, to make recordings. 'We couldn't have got on without the missionaries,' she often said. 'They've been the ones to help us, advise us, get us in touch with informants.' But on this occasion, to her surprise, she received no replies.

'Things are very touchy in Ethiopia,' she was told. 'The missionaries there have to walk very carefully. The Emperor is surrounded by people who are very antagonistic. His hands are tied. It wouldn't be at all a good time to go. Very dangerous indeed even to suggest getting in touch with tribes-people and making recordings in their languages. You'd be under suspicion straight away, and so would the people you tried to work with.'

It would be foolhardy to go in the face of such reports, she knew. She would not only endanger her own project, but jeopardise the well-established work of others. Yet the urge to go persisted, and with it the most preposterous idea that had yet come to her. Not only did she want to go to Ethiopia. She wanted to gain an audience with the Emperor himself, and ask permission to make recordings in his country. She could not dismiss the conviction that it would happen.

Without an invitation from so much as one person in Ethiopia, however, how could she go? If the Lord wanted her to go, then she was sure He would see to it that she received an invitation.

An invitation came. It was from a missionary couple she had known in north India. They had recently transferred to Ethiopia, and having only just arrived, not knowing the sensitive political situation, replied to her letter giving her a cordial invitation to come.

Joy was in Nairobi when their letter arrived. She had been ill, on and off, for some time, but that could not be allowed to hinder her now. If a door opened in Ethiopia she was intended to go through it. Ann and Sanna, whose confidence in her spiritual discernment had increased during the years they were together, were prepared to back her up in this decision. Funds were very low, but they pooled their resources and had just enough to pay for the air ticket to Addis Ababa. None of them had much left in their purses after that, but their faith was high. Experience had proved that God's provision came from very unexpected quarters, but it always arrived on time. So Joy set off to go at last to the country that had first drawn out her desire to become a missionary.

The short time she spent in Addis Ababa on that occasion was one of the most memorable of her life. She never forgot it. Some of the details were etched on her memory with such clarity that she could relate them vividly twenty years later.

First there was the arrival at the airport. To her amazement, instead of only one missionary to meet her, there were representatives of about five different missions. They had come to welcome her. They knew of her work, had actually received Gospel Recordings records in Amharic and several of the larger tribal languages, made outside the country and then sent in. The records had been an immediate success, evoking an unprecedented response, until the Minister of Education had banned them. Things were rather tense at present, the missionaries intimated. They had been told to destroy all the records. It was better not to talk too freely. But they were delighted to meet her, and hoped she would speak at their united prayer meeting, which happened to fall due that very afternoon.

Cautiously she outlined her desire – to make recordings in the tribal languages of Ethiopia. As things stood, they knew it was undesirable even to make the attempt, though no-one said so, but after the meeting one of the men came up to speak to her. He had something else on his mind.

'Miss Ridderhof, I'm so glad to meet you,' he said. 'We take an offering each week at this meeting, and some time ago took one for you and your two friends. I'm the treasurer, as it happens, but I didn't know whereabouts in Africa you were, so I couldn't send it to you. Would you mind taking it now?'

Joy, whose mind had flashed more than once to the emptiness of her purse, and the embarrassment it could be in a strange city, assured him that she would not mind in the least taking it now. *Thank you, Lord,* she breathed inwardly. *Now I'll be able to pay for my board.* It was a relief, and she could turn her attention to the main purpose of her visit. She wanted to obtain permission from the Emperor himself to make recordings in his country. She wanted to meet the Emperor himself.

The missionaries shook their heads dubiously. It could not be done. Missionaries do not usually move in such exalted circles. But one man at the prayer meeting that afternoon had an idea.

'Your own Ambassador could help you,' he said. 'If you can meet Dr. Simonson and present your case, he might be able to obtain an audience for you with His Majesty.' So the necessary arrangements were made, and after visiting the United States Ambassador a time was fixed when he would accompany her to the palace of his Imperial Majesty, Haile Selassie, Lion of the Tribe of Judah, Emperor of Ethiopia.

Joy left the Embassy that day with her heart singing. 'Ethiopia shall soon stretch out her hands unto God,' she had read in Psalm 68 a short time before, and it took on an intimate meaning. It did not refer to something remote, allegorical, far away, but to living Ethiopians – now. The pagan tribes would soon be hearing in their own tongues the wonderful works of God. She wanted to be alone, so went into the little chapel on the mission compound where she was staying. But she was too excited to pray. She could do nothing else but praise, and sitting down at the little organ played and sang hymns with all her might until she had no breath left.

But there were practical things to attend to. If she had taken trouble to be correctly attired for a buffet tea and reception in a hotel in London, how much more attention should be paid to appearing before an Emperor. She hadn't the right clothes! What she lacked, however, others readily supplied, bag, gloves, shoes, and finally a most suitable wrap which she saw someone wearing at the missionary prayer meeting, and asked outright if she might borrow, since she was to have an audience with the Emperor the next day. The owner took it off then and there, and handed it to her.

So the day came when, sitting beside the United States Ambassador, grave and dignified in his formal suit with swallow-tail coat, she was driven in the Embassy car to the palace. As they passed smoothly through the gates she saw the lions pacing to and fro in their ornamental cages. She had heard them roaring night after night, and the sight of them increased her sense of awe. She shuddered.

But now they were at the palace, alighting from the car, mounting the steps where tall, dark-skinned Ethiopians stood on guard. They were greeted by an official in western clothes, the Minister of Pen, who would act as interpreter. Now she must remember exactly what to do. Bow low, walk slowly towards the Emperor, never turn your face away from him for a moment, bow again ... She saw him at the end of the long, vast hall, an erect, dignified little figure in his kingly gown. He stood to receive them out of respect for the Ambassador walking beside her. She was conscious of two or three other men with him, dressed in western clothes, but kept her eyes on the Emperor. After the Ambassador had presented his gifts and made a few preliminary remarks, he came to the purpose of the visit, and Joy had her opportunity. The Emperor looked at her and nodded, waiting for her to speak.

'Your Majesty,' she said. 'We have made records based on the Bible in other countries, so that people who cannot read

can hear and understand. Now we would like to make them
with nationals in your country, in tribal languages as well as in
Amharic . . .' Everything she said was interpreted to him, and
although it was well-known that having spent years of exile in
England he understood and spoke English, his replies were
made in Amharic and translated back to her. Yes, he believed
in the Bible. He had arranged for the Bible to be translated into
intelligible Amharic, which the people could understand. Yes,
he was pleased to have recordings made in languages of people
who could not read. He not only nodded his approval, he
spoke it to her in English. When the interview concluded,
conscious of the spoken word of the Emperor granting her
request, she backed slowly away with the Ambassador,
bowing carefully, all down the great hall until eventually she
reached the entrance and turned round. The Minister of Pen
was there, and she asked,

'Will you please implement this permission.'

He looked at her coldly. 'What permission?'

She knew then that the door which seemed to be opening
was still fast closed. There would be no written permission and
no recordings. The spoken word within the palace meant
nothing without the written word of confirmation, and the men
standing silently round the Emperor would support the powerful Minister of Education.

There was nothing more she could do. Yes, there was one
thing. She could still rejoice! 'Let's just rejoice! It seems
disappointing, but in my heart there's real hope that this thing
will work out for good. The Lord's given me Psalm 68, and I
know He's going to do some marvellous things. I trust Him,
and I'll just rejoice!'

She went back to Nairobi, and with Ann and Sanna
continued their journeyings through Africa. If the year 1955
had contained the perplexity of the Ethiopian denial of access,
it ended with some very significant statistics in the Gospel
Recordings records. The one million mark in the number of
records sent out since the inception of the work was passed,
and new languages captured were coming in from the field
recordists in Africa and Asia at the rate of nearly one a day.

The grand total of languages and dialects recorded had risen to 1,401 by the end of the year.

One thousand, four hundred and one. It would have been a round figure of one thousand and four hundred had it not been that the Trio in Africa, while in Tanganyika heard quite accidentally of a little tribe of pygmies that was dying out.

'The Wakindiga – oh, you'll never get them. They live in the Yaida Swamps, and roam from place to place, you never know where they'll turn up next. They're very elusive, and afraid of white people. Very few of them anyway – maybe only about 500. No-one will ever learn their language, of course . . .'

The basic facts which would have been sufficient to deter most people from interrupting a carefully planned itinerary to attempt to reach so small, so insignificant a little branch of the human family were precisely the type that would have the opposite effect on Joy. She always had a special compassion for the by-passed. Back in Marcala her visiting often took her to one home where a deformed, mentally deficient child was the first person for whom she looked and with whom she spent time before going to teach the other members. As a teen-ager she stayed away from a picnic she would have loved to join in, because she knew a lonely woman was dying of cancer in a hospital, and might need her. The thought of that shy, timid pygmy race, quietly dying out with no knowledge of the Shepherd who leaves the ninety and nine in the fold to go seeking that which is lost, was too much for her. As she and Ann and Sanna worked away making recordings of the nine other language groups in the area, their most persistent urgent prayer to God, and their most consistent oft-repeated request to man was concerning the Wakindiga.

'We *must* get this language. It's small, isolated people like this that can be missed entirely unless they have the Gospel presented to them in their very own tongue. They are our priority for records, because none of the usual means of evangelism can reach them. Do you know anyone who is in touch with them? Anyone who can help us reach them?'

Finally information came through and contact was made with a missionary living on the western border of the Yaida

Swamp. He was the one in the best position to get in contact with the Wakindiga, and he was the one who a short time later sent a runner with the message that on Monday morning next three Wakindiga from the forest would be at his mission station, ready to help in making recordings. To ensure that they arrived he went and fetched them himself — three little brown men in tattered shirts and pants, carrying bows and arrows. Communication was slow, but after two and a half days the recordings had been made.

Then followed one of the oustanding experiences of the Trio's years in Africa. Carrying the recorder the missionary living by the Yaida Swamp led Joy and her two companions up to the pygmy encampment on a rock-strewn hillside where the Wakindiga were to hear the message from God that came out of the 'talking box'. There, under the starlit African sky, the diminutive bush-dwellers heard for the first time that Jesus, from Heaven, had died to open for them the gate of everlasting life. And it was the voice of their own tribal chief who proclaimed it.

When the tape was sent back to Los Angeles for the processes that would eventually transform it into little round discs for the Wakindiga, it was marked as Top Priority. 'These sort of people must come first — they mustn't be missed out.'

Throughout the year that followed her trip to Addis Ababa, working through Congo, Kenya, Tanganyika, Joy turned again and again to Psalm 68. God had spoken to her through that Psalm. 'Ethiopia shall soon stretch out her hands unto God.' She couldn't and she wouldn't let that promise go. There were other verses in the Psalm that impressed her, too. 'God shall wound the head of his enemies, and the hairy scalp of such an one as goeth on still in his trespasses.' She didn't know what it might mean, but it impressed her. Most of all, however, she noticed the calls to praise. 'Sing unto God, sing praises to His name . . . rejoice before Him . . . rejoice before God; yea, let them exceedingly rejoice.' On the face of it, there seemed little to rejoice in over the Ethiopian episode, but rejoice she would, and see what God would do.

Then she went down with sciatica. It was excruciatingly painful, and she had only partially recovered when they set off back across Congo. Their visas had nearly expired, and they dared not wait any longer to make for the border. Sanna was ill by this time, lying in the back of the jeep, but there was nothing for it — they must go on. There was another reason. News had arrived from Ethiopia, and it was cautiously hopeful. There might be an opportunity now for recordings to be made in the country.

It was enough for Joy. Ethiopia was the target now. But before they got to the border they stopped at an Africa Inland Mission hospital, where Dr. Carl Becker after two days of untiring efforts to bring about Sanna's recovery, announced, 'She is dismissed! She can go on.' What a relief! Instead of having to take her back to the States, they could all go on to Ethiopia. So over they went through Uganda into Kenya, to Nairobi and the Ethiopian Consulate.

They had made their application for visas ahead of time, but wondered whether they would be allowed into the country. Their reception at the Consulate did little to reassure them. It was grudging, to say the least, but they were told,

'Your passports are out there on the table.' So out they went, and looking at their passports they saw they had permission to go into Ethiopia and remain there for three months. They could scarcely believe it was true, for the time usually granted was a matter of days.

They took the plane to Addis Ababa. When they left, three months later, they had obtained recordings in over thirty languages.

There had undoubtedly been some changes, Joy observed, and enquired what had happened to bring them about.

It had to do with the Minister of Education, she was told. He had been the one who had most rigidly obstructed things, and it had been at his order that the records already in the country had been banned. A mental condition had developed which made it necessary for him to go abroad for treatment. Now that he was out of the country restrictions were being removed.

Joy looked reflectively at Psalm 68, verse 21. 'God shall wound the head of his enemies, and the hairy scalp of such an one as goeth on still in his trespasses.' A mental condition was certainly something in the head, she thought, and under a hairy scalp. It seemed to fit the case.

9

Sealed Orders

THOSE WHO BELIEVE God has a plan for the life of everyone who receives Christ Jesus as Saviour and Lord have ample evidence to support their claim in the apparently unpredictable travels of Joy Ridderhof. Particularly during the formative years of Gospel Recordings so many incidents occurred which led to people whose talents and achievements were to have a vital effect on the work that it would be difficult to doubt that a Master Mind had prepared the sealed orders under which she travelled.

The Nagra story is a case in point. The Nagra, a highly sensitive, light yet remarkably strong tape recorder came on the market in 1958, but it came too slowly to supply the immediate need. It was so light in weight, so sensitive in reception, yet would stand up to such rough treatment that reporters and television newsmen were falling over each other to obtain models. The price was high, but they were undeterred. The Nagra was worth it. They made their applications early, badgered the distributors, waited impatiently for months before eventually holding their own Nagra in their own hands. Yet at this very time Gospel Recordings, an inconspicuous little organisation the national mass media had never heard of, was receiving a steady supply of the coveted machines just as they were needed.

This is how it came about. On Joy's first visit to England she was talking to Livingston Hogg one day and in the course of conversation he said, 'If you want a really good battery-operated recording machine, the best in the world will be coming on the market soon. It's just the thing you need. It's called the Nagra. The inventor is a man named Kudelsky. He lives in Switzerland.'

Immediately she fastened on the information. Right from the start the recording machine had been the mechanical key to her work. Upon it everything depended. All the careful preparation of scripts, all the arrangements with interpreters, all the arduous travel produced no recordings if the machine went wrong. She was always on the alert to learn of new and improved methods, of models that were lighter to carry, easier to work, less liable to breakdowns. She made a note of the Nagra, therefore, and the name of the inventor, but apart from that could do nothing else except pray, as she frequently prayed, for better machines.

It so happened that she had arranged to stay in Switzerland for a few days on her way to Africa. The Nagra was on her mind and its name on her tongue, and the name of its inventor, too. She did not know where he lived, but the Divine Secret Service was at work again. She found she had come to stay in a home where her host not only knew where the inventor lived, but was personally acquainted with him. Since he lived not very far away an interview with him could be arranged if Miss Ridderhof would like to meet him, he said.

Of all the wonderful things! There was no-one in the whole of Switzerland, or in Europe, or, for that matter, in the whole world, that Miss Ridderhof more desired to meet just then than the inventor of the Nagra! A short time later she found herself sitting and talking to him.

'It isn't completed yet,' she was told. 'It must be foolproof, able to stand up to very hard wear — it's tested by being dropped from the air by parachute. It'll be mainly used by reporters.' The matter of distributors came up, and Joy suggested Livingston Hogg for England. 'Oh, I've got twenty people who would take it on,' observed the inventor. There would be no lack of people eager to dispose of the machine. Then he asked, quite casually, 'How many machines would you be wanting?'

She had not expected the question. With her intimate and varied experience of recording machines she knew that this new one could have a transforming effect on the work of the field recordists. But she also knew how much each machine was to cost. Its price would be approximately that of a new saloon car.

'How many machines would you be wanting?' The question remained suspended in air, waiting for an answer, and she knew she must say something.

'Twenty-four,' she replied. She had no reason for giving that number. On the strength of her bank balance she was in no position to order even one, yet here she was talking in terms of the equivalent of a fleet of twenty-four new saloon cars! The words were out before she had time to think, based on no wise assessments of her own, but in the months and years to come she was to realise how accurate and significant they were. When the precious and rare Nagras appeared one by one, with eager buyers clamouring to obtain them, those two words 'twenty-four' formed the basis on which Gospel Recordings Inc. could claim to have placed an order which put it high on the priority list of customers to be supplied. And since Livingston Hogg was, after all, appointed distributor of the Nagra in England, he was in a good position to ensure that the order was fulfilled when required.

The first of the twenty-four Nagras was bought by Sanna Barlow, for her forthcoming trip to South Africa. It had been arranged that she should go there to do some recording and on her way to England to pick it up she was asked by a wealthy businessman in Florida if she could meet him in New York. He was on the Board of the Columbia Bible College, had become interested in Gospel Recordings, and having heard her speak about it had something he wanted to ask her.

Sanna was somewhat alarmed at the prospect of dining with him. He was very knowledgeable about machines, and she was afraid he wanted to ask her about the Phonette which Stuart Mill had just produced. Everyone was very excited about the Phonette, and it was wonderful to have a motorless, hand-wind gramophone that couldn't go wrong. When it came to explaining how it worked, however, Sanna knew she wouldn't have the right answers. She was not mechanically minded. She had lived with tape recorders for years and she knew how to work them when they were in order, but when they weren't and had to be taken to pieces to discover where the fault lay, Sanna was admittedly at a loss. True, there had been one occasion in India, when she had discovered what had baffled even the technician, but it was so unusual none of the Trio ever forgot it. It was the highlight of her experience along that line, 'The time Sanna found what was wrong'. What especially appealed to her about the Nagra, she said with her slow smile, was that it claimed to be foolproof.

'I do hope Mr. Rossi won't ask me anything about mechanism,' she thought apprehensively. It would be so much easier if his questions had to do with her visit to South Africa, or the book she was writing, or G.R. policies.

As it turned out, however, the only question to which he really wanted an answer had nothing to do with machines, books, travels or policies. It took her completely by surprise, and she did not reply in a hurry. The time came, however, when she had to let Joy know that when she had completed her assignment in South Africa she would be getting married, as she had accepted Anthony Rossi's proposal.

There were times in Joy's experience when she found it very difficult to rejoice, and this was one of them. Sanna to marry Anthony Rossi! Not only did that mean the loss of a fellow worker who had become unusually dear to her, but it meant also that so far from the number of field recordists being increased, it was being reduced. But if one rejoiced only when things went well, where was the evidence of faith? Real trust was proved by rejoicing that God's plan was best, even when it went contrary to what one had expected.

The period since returning from the five and a half years of recording with Ann and Sanna had not been easy. After the first glow of delight at being back at the heart of Gospel Recordings, where her own home was, she became conscious of an indefinable change in the atmosphere there. Marie's affection was unchanged, but she was now the mother of a teen-age daughter, Professor Ridderhof had died, so home was not quite the same. This had not disturbed her so much as the realisation that her own position in the organisation that had grown up around her was not quite the same, either. Everything ran very smoothly and efficiently, requests for records were flooding in and the orders being executed promptly. There was no cause for anxiety along that line, and she would have found it difficult to explain why it was that instead of being happy as before in the heart of her Gospel Recordings family, she felt uneasy. She was still the Director, but she was no longer needed, and there were occasions when she wondered if she was even wanted, whether some, at any rate, would not be better pleased if she were away. She was oppressed.

Ann and Sanna had felt equally disquieted, but for them the situation had been different. Ann's home was with her sisters in the rambling old family home at Inglewood, miles away from Witmer Street, while Sanna's mother lived far away in Tennessee. When the work of recording or speaking at meetings did not claim them they could gravitate naturally to their own families, away from the place that somehow was not the 'home' they had so often talked about when on their travels. Joy had no other place to go to. Eventually she purchased an old caravan which was placed in the garden of a friend, on a hilltop in South Pasadena. Here she would retire to read and write and pray. It was a relief to be there, away from the feeling of tension that so strangely gripped her now when she was at Witmer Street. Another matter was constantly on her mind, too.

The most vital part of the work was not progressing. The output of records was steadily increasing, the Australian and English branches were growing, there was encouraging news of the possibility of another branch being established in India. Gospel Recordings was being consolidated, but there was an ominous slowing down in the addition of new languages. The primary purpose of conveying the Gospel to those who would otherwise have no way of hearing it in the tongue they could understand was not being achieved. The outstanding need was for new recordists. Vaughn Collins, after a brief furlough, was preparing to go to South America to capture the voices of its innumerable Indian tribes hidden in vast primeval forests and dry deserts, but the hope that a team of young men would be forthcoming to join him had not been realised. By March 1958, John van Kampen alone had come forward with his offer to give one year to the recording work before returning to his own field with The Evangelical Alliance Mission. There were no more full-time recordists for G.R.

Then had come the evidence that physically she was ill. Visits to the doctor and hospital confirmed that she had cancer, and must undergo major surgery.

If the news alarmed others, it disturbed her very little. She almost welcomed it. Here was an opportunity to rejoice in the face of something tangible, very much easier and more straightforward than rejoicing when opposition was invisible, imperceptible, and could not be given a name. She went into hospital quite cheerfully, and when it was all over, reviewing her experiences, the one that had probably impressed her most was the telephone call she received from Herman Dyk just about the time she had decided she would refuse to have any more radium treatment. Herman had something on his mind that he must pass on.

'Joy,' he said firmly. 'I want to tell you that I don't believe you ought to have any more radium treatment. I feel the Lord has given me the assurance He'll complete your cure without it.'

'Oh, Herman, I'm so glad you've called,' she replied. 'Because that's just what the Lord has been telling me!' If the doctors shook their heads dubiously at the time, there was nothing they could say against the decision eighteen years later, when she had travelled round the world three or four times, and was even now rarely at home for more than two weeks at a time.

'God has proven again that our "light affliction" is but our servant to bring about an eternal weight of glory,' she wrote to her friends when she was out of hospital. 'Only Eternity will reveal all the blessings which resulted from it, but I carry many of them in my heart. My thanksgivings are many. For the splendid hospital care; for the free professional services of doctors; for two special nurses who watched beside me the first night after surgery . . . I am now resting in the home of friends in La Mesa, California, situated in an avocado grove on a beautiful hill top site. I am able to be up a good part of every day, even to take short walks. My hostess, who is a nurse, is amazed at my progress.' She was planning to go on a light speaking tour next month, she announced, and concluded her letter with the words, 'Truly I believe my best days lie ahead. Promises, hopes and expectations for the future abound. I feel as though God had given me a new commission, and I eagerly look forward to its fulfilment.'

She did not specify precisely what she believed the new commission to be, or whether it was, in fact, a renewal of the one she had already received. To proclaim the simple message of salvation in every tongue under heaven was still her absorbing desire. This was the purpose above all for which she lived.

It could not be achieved, however, without the addition of more field recordists. Twenty years had passed since the making of the first simple Spanish record, and in that time nearly two thousand languages had been captured. But the deeper the recordists penetrated, the more strange tongues and voices were being discovered, fresh seams of humanity like silver waiting to be mined from the dark earth. If she and Ann and the others could continue for another twenty years with the same physical and mental strength they had already brought to the task they could not hope to reach them all. The whole process must be speeded up, and as she thought and prayed about it the idea was conceived in her mind that was to prove more effective than any other in recruiting young men and women whose health, dedication and freedom from family ties would fit them for the demanding work of field recording.

The idea was simple enough. During the long summer vacation many university and college students, eager young Christians among them, had time on their hands. Why not provide them with the opportunity to take a practical share in the day to day work at Gospel Recordings in Los Angeles? Let them learn some of the skills of recording and editing in the studio, take a share in the work in factory, offices, packing department. Their help would boost areas where a backlog had to be made up, and fill the gaps left by the regular workers going on holiday. And what might not result in the way of vision being given of the world-wide task still to be completed, and guidance at the most crucial time in young lives which are waiting a call from the Master?

Joy was full of enthusiasm for the idea. She visited a number of colleges, ardently presenting the possibility inherent in the unique techniques of Gospel Recordings — that of proclaiming the Gospel to every man in his own tongue. Was not the Apocalyptic vision of the praising multitudes gathered from all nations and kindreds and peoples and tongues to have its fulfilment? Yet how could they be there without faith in Christ, and how could they have faith in Him they had never heard of? And how could they hear without a preacher? Now, in these very days, the means had been supplied whereby they could hear. Little black discs spinning on hand-wind gramophones could be the preachers. The return of the Lord from heaven could be hastened, for He Himself had said, 'This gospel of the Kingdom shall be preached in all the world for a witness to all nations; and then shall the end come'. It was all very practical, and the positive proof she could produce of the effectiveness of the records added to the inspirational value of what she had to say.

A man in Mexico was saved through hearing the records — now he had led fifty others to Christ.

About three hundred people in one area in India were converted, mainly through gramophone evangelism. Missionaries visiting Angola reported having met people who had been brought to the Lord through the records. An illiterate Brazilian Christian took Gospel records and went where no missionary had ever been. Five souls were won to Christ there. A man in the Philippines travelled for twelve hours to hear more about the Lord Jesus, of whom he had heard from 'a big box that talked'. Tribespeople sat through the night listening to the

records that spoke their own language. Day after day letters
were being received asking for more records because 'they are
reaching those who might otherwise never hear'.

Beaming as she reiterated her favourite theme of rejoicing in
everything, Joy held her audiences breathlessly attentive, and
now that she had something positive to suggest she was even
more enthusiastic. There was something really worthwhile that
young people could do in their summer vacation. Come to
Gospel Recordings as an Interim Co-Labourer! See things
from the inside, attend the staff discussions and prayer meetings, take part in the work, speed up the output of records to
the uttermost ends of the earth!

The I.C.L. project was launched in the summer of 1959.
Most of the young people who attended that session eventually
became field recordists.

Meanwhile, Joy set out on a trip that was to take her round
the world. The main purpose was to discover where were the
greatest needs and opportunities for making recordings, and
also to visit the flourishing branch in Australia where a factory
had been built on a five and a half acre plot of land outside
Sydney. Not only records, but 'talking boxes' were being
produced. They were called Phonettes. The idea of a motorless
gramophone Joy had implanted in Stuart Mill's mind had
become a reality, and no matter how irregularly the handle
was turned the record rotated at the required seventy-eight
revolutions per minute. Not that Stuart Mill was completely
satisfied something even simpler couldn't be invented, something cheaper to produce and easier to pack. But nearly ten
years were to pass before the combined experiments of Gospel
Recordings inventors eventually produced a record player
consisting of three pieces of cardboard and a needle, so easily
worked that even the most primitive jungle dweller was not
baffled.

From Australia Joy moved on through Papua, New Guinea,
countries of south-east Asia – to India.

In some ways the fortnight she spent there was the most
memorable of the whole nine-months trip. India – the country
had never been far from her mind for six years, and now she

was there again, hoping to see the culmination of many prayers. Even before leaving Australia she had been encouraged by the response of one young man to her suggestion that he should go to India to set up a Gospel Recordings factory. David Macnaughtan had been aware that the call of God lay behind her request, and was prepared to obey when the time was ripe. The fortnight she would spend with Elvie Nicoll in India was to pave the way for him.

It was in 1954, during her first visit to Australia, that Joy first met the hospitable Elvie Nicoll, well-known in Melbourne for her varied Christian activities in the city. The two women, about the same age and with a similar outlook on life, immediately became friendly, and on her second visit to Melbourne Joy stayed with her. The visit lasted several days, and their routine always commenced in the same way – early morning devotions in their adjoining rooms. Their relationship was very informal, so when Joy, one morning, called, 'Elvie!' Elvie responded immediately, 'Hello, Joy! What is it?' The reply she received was so startling that she could not believe she had understood aright.

'Elvie, would you consider working overseas with Gospel Recordings?'

Elvie gasped.

'I beg your pardon?' she said, although she knew she had heard perfectly. Joy repeated the question, and Elvie walked into her room to continue the discussion face to face.

'But Joy,' she protested, 'the Lord has given me all this work here in Melbourne!' She didn't mention that she was over fifty, had given up the idea of being a missionary thirty years ago when, after training to be one, ill health had closed the door, and that she was now thoroughly established in her life in Melbourne. Those were not, after all, primary considerations, but the work she was doing for God was. 'How could I leave it to go overseas?'

'I'm not asking you to do it,' said Joy. 'I'm only asking you to pray about it. Will you do that? Because I'm going to!' Rather light-heartedly Elvie agreed to do so, and to her surprise what had seemed like an exciting but most unlikely suggestion deepened into a conviction that this was, in fact, the very thing she should do — sell up her home, relinquish her various commitments in Melbourne, and launch out as a Gospel Recordings field worker with the aim of establishing bases in Asian countries and then move on. Once assured that the call of God had come to her she did not hesitate and in June 1956 set off to represent Gospel Recordings in the Far East.

'How do I go about it?' she had asked Joy, and the answer she had received was simply, 'Oh, gossip Gospel Recordings, take meetings ...' with an airy wave of the hand. 'The Lord will tell you what to do!'

As a Director Joy did not hamper people with a superfluity of instructions, but she made it very clear to Whom they must look for their guidance.

The experiences of Elvie along this line would be sufficient to fill a book. Before she started out from Australia she had taken as her personal promise the words, originally spoken to Moses, 'Behold, I send an angel before thee, to keep thee in the way, and to bring thee unto the place which I have prepared'. The assurance had proved as reliable to her as it had proved to Joy and Ann years before, when they set off for Mindoro in the Philippines. First she went to Singapore and established a records distribution centre there, making the Overseas Missionary Fellowship her headquarters. J. Oswald Sanders, the General Director, had been a fellow student of hers in Bible School days and he and his wife were like brother and sister to her as she launched out in her new work.

Then she moved on to India. A year or two later, in January, 1960, she was in Calcutta, waiting to meet Joy off the plane and start looking for a site for a Gospel Recordings factory somewhere in India. Preparations were complete. She had been in Delhi to try and find out how to get a factory started, and had been promised help by Small Scale Industries once she had obtained Government permission to do this in India. Then she had gained an interview with a Member of Parliament who had instructed her to put in writing what Gospel Recordings was and what it wanted to do. This she had done, and now all that remained was to find a suitable site in whatever city Joy believed was the right one.

So Joy arrived for the second time in India. Six years previously she had stood with Ann and Sanna and their mountain of baggage, bewildered by the noise and the dark-skinned porters whose instructions they could not understand, and who disappeared into the throng of people with their precious suitcases and recorders balanced precariously on turbaned heads. The panic-stricken rush to follow those suit-cases bobbing up and down above the sea of heads was something she never forgot, nor the oppressive sense of the enormity of the task to which the three of them had come. Ever since that time she had been praying that God would open effective doors for Gospel Recordings in India and now here was Elvie, smilingly welcoming her, efficiently seeing her through Customs, dealing with all the business, and ready to show her the lists of missionaries and Indian Christians who were distributing the records being imported from Los Angeles and players from Australia. The demand was so great, and the duty charged on the records so high, that it had been decided the records for India must be pressed in the country itself. That was why Elvie had urged Joy to come at this time. She wanted Joy, as Director, to take the responsibility for choosing the location of the factory. Should it be in Delhi or Bombay, or Calcutta or Madras — or where?

'Bangalore,' said Joy. She had asked God to guide her, and the more she prayed about it the more deeply Bangalore was imprinted on her mind, so to Bangalore they went to look for property.

Elvie was not without experience regarding the purchase of property, but she had never met anyone who set about it in quite the same way as Joy, whose mind leapt ahead with a fine disregard for legal restrictions and municipal laws to fasten enthusiastically on a variety of properties, all of which proved to be unsuitable. Elvie never doubted the wisdom of Joy's choice of Bangalore, and later events confirmed the Divine direction she had received. After a fortnight of seeking property with her, however, Elvie came to the quiet conclusion that God did not always work through flashes of inspiration, and that her own more normal methods, though slower, might move more surely than Joy's when it came to matters of real estate. Joy left for Africa before anything was settled, and eventually Elvie heard of the Ebenezer Church Compound in a residential area near the old British barracks and race-course. Here she met John and Lillian Gray from Canada.

John Gray had accepted the invitation to become pastor of the old British military church named Ebenezer when it was at its lowest ebb, with less than a dozen members. The congregation could offer him no salary, only somewhere to live – an old colonial-type bungalow with large dark rooms and deep balconies, situated in three acres of ground that looked like a jungle. Fellow missionaries had warned him he was taking on a white elephant, and that he would end up broken-hearted with his life's goals crushed. But since all his inner convictions led him to the conclusion that God wanted him in the Ebenezer Church he accepted the invitation, and by the time Elvie Nicoll appeared on the scene the congregation was steadily increasing, although he hadn't had time to do much about the jungle. When Elvie expressed her need for property on which to build a factory and studio for Gospel Recordings he saw a way of subduing part of the jungle, and negotiations with the Church's Board of Trustees resulted in Gospel Recordings obtaining a fifty years' lease of land on which to build. And as there was far more room in the parsonage than the Grays needed, part of it could be loaned to the G.R. staff.

So was established the Gospel Recordings branch in India.

10

The Peak Years

TO BE A field recordist you must be tough. It isn't only that
you must be tough physically, able to endure long hours of
hard travelling, uncomfortable nights in strange beds, un-
palatable food difficult to digest, extremes of temperature
ranging from below zero to one hundred degrees in the shade,
and the sort of constitution that comes up sturdily after the
bouts of malaria, dysentery, and fevers that will almost
certainly assail you in your travels. You must be tough
mentally, able to concentrate for hours on end, able to grasp
the techniques of linguistics as well as of sensitive recording
machines, able to discern when what you've said has been
inadvertently twisted by the interpreter to say what you did
not mean. You must be tough spiritually, too, able to overcome the depression that will attack you when things go
wrong, able to wait patiently through hours, days, even weeks
when the arrangements you thought you'd made don't
materialise, or when the tribe you thought had been located for
you melts into the jungle or the desert — or when you find
yourself trudging from one government department to another
in a country whose language you don't understand trying to
obtain permission to bring in your equipment when you enter,
or to be allowed to take it with you when you leave.

And you must be tough emotionally, not easily moved, not
quickly deflected from your course by the gentle insistent call
of natural affection . . .

'So it's no marriage, no engagement, no understanding with

any girl during the first five-year term,' said Joy to the young man who stood with her at the airport as she waited for the call to board her plane. 'If you feel the Lord has called you to field recording with G.R., you must understand our regulation. If you accept the call, you must accept the restriction.'

'Yes, I see,' he said, looking straight ahead of him. He did not speak lightly, and Joy understood why. She glanced at him and continued, 'If you accept, I would recommend that you break off immediately with your girl friend.' Then she added a piece of advice.

'Don't take time to reason it out with her, or break it to her gradually. If you try to do it that way, it will only complicate the matter.'

On the face of it, it sounded hard, but as she spoke something happened which he never forgot.

'I experienced in that moment an infilling of the grace of God that was unique in any experience I've ever had, even since,' he said fifteen years later. 'I found myself willing and even believing that it was best this way.'

When the confirming grace of Divine authority accompanied so much of what she said and did, it is not surprising that Joy was a leader even young men could follow.

The fact that she only expected of others the sort of renunciations she herself had made had something to do with the quality of her leadership. The young men and women who came to the Interim Co-Labourer sessions at Gospel Recordings saw the plain little attic room that was still her only home, observed the way she came into the dining room for meals just like anyone else, and took her share in serving food and washing up, observed the old, rattling car in which she drove, and drew their own conclusions. This Director appeared to require no special privileges to attend her position.

One young couple who joined the work were vividly reminded of an interview they had had some time previously with the Director of another Christian organisation. They had just completed their Bible School training, and he had arranged to take them out to dinner to explain the job he might be prepared to offer them. They were somewhat dismayed when they saw their prospective employer drive up in a new white Cadillac. As the position they were applying for was to represent the charity, and most of their time would be spent in raising funds for it, they did not feel very happy about that sumptuous, sparkling car. During the interview they could not disguise their reaction to that new Cadillac. They'd feel rather uneasy if they knew the money they were raising went on things like that ... They and the Director parted with polite smiles and the mutual, if unspoken agreement that they were not the sort of people he was looking for.

Joy's unconscious example extended far beyond a simple style of living at home. Those who prepared to launch out as 'fielders', going to strange countries and untried situations, were well aware that no-one knew more about the hardships to be endured than their leader. Her own experiences made her very sensitive to the difficulties they encountered, and there were times when she seemed to be aware that they were in distress although she was thousands of miles away and had no direct communication. David Macnaughtan, during his first year in India, fell sick with hepatitis and was extremely ill. Within the week, before any news of his condition could have reached Joy, he received a letter from her saying, 'David, I know something is wrong, and I just want you to know that I am praying for you.' Such sensitivity and evidence of intimate concern endeared her fellow workers to her, and inspired their confidence. If the instructions she gave were not always clear, there was never any doubt of the sincerity and warmth of her affection. She wrote frequently to them, wherever she happened to be, rattling off letters in as chatty a way as if she were there talking to them.

'Dear, dear young people, I love you very very much,' she wrote to the I.C.L.s one Christmas. 'You came to us and helped us and we are grateful to our Heavenly Father for you. We have made a list of all the I.C.L.s who have been with us — I believe there are forty of you now. We are interested in each one of you and are praying that God will lead you into the place of His will. I will be remembering you by name before the throne at this season.'

'Are you practising rejoicing?' she asked. 'Remember —
make a victory of it by rejoicing! The hard things are good
rejoicing practice. That thing that has been your hardest trial,
that disappointment, that disillusionment, that thing that
seemed such a tragedy, that biting experience doubtless will
prove to be something that you will thank God for with all
your heart when you see His purpose in permitting it. I'm not
young, and I can talk from knowledge.'

She was over sixty when she wrote that letter, and at the
height of her mental and spiritual powers, with her vitality
undiminished. With her wide and intimate knowledge of
missionary situations throughout the world she was frequently
invited to speak at important conferences, the recognised
founder-director of a unique organisation that was growing
rapidly. In addition to the centres in Australia, England and
India, others were being established. One had come into being
in South Africa as a result of Sanna Barlow's months there to
make recordings. In Mexico Herman Dyk was running a
Gospel Recordings factory, and in Canada a Member of
Parliament had added to his activities by becoming Chairman
of the Gospel Recordings branch he himself had brought into
being.

Dr. Robert Thompson had had a colourful career. In the
Canadian Air Force during the Second World War, he had
been expecting an overseas posting on the eve of D-Day, but
he hadn't expected it to be to Ethiopia. The Emperor Haile
Selassie, back at last in his own country after his years of exile,
had appealed for men, since so many of his own army and air
force officers had been lost in the Fascist conquest. His appeal,
made through the senior R.A.F. Chaplain and Dr. R. V.
Bingham, General Director of the Sudan Interior Mission,
resulted in the young Canadian finding himself re-organising
the Imperial Ethiopian Air Force as First Commander of the
training programme. After the war he remained in Ethiopia as
Associate Deputy Minister in a Government Department, then
leaving Government service joined the Sudan Interior Mission
to head their educational programme. His responsibilities had
taken him to the south of the country, where large concen-

trations of the Arussi Galla tribe claimed his attention. The Arussi Galla tribe didn't really welcome government plans to improve their way of life. They preferred their own semi-nomadic existence. They hadn't welcomed missionaries, either, having killed a couple of them in 1936. They weren't going to be easy to reach with the Gospel but Thompson, who had spent many hours with them over their camp fires, saw in a flash what a talking box that spoke their own language might accomplish among them. He had supported Joy's project from the time he heard about it, and had seen the effectiveness of the records as the spearhead of evangelism in the tribe he particularly loved. Hundreds had embraced the Christian faith as a result of them, and on his return to Canada he determined to promote Gospel Recordings in his own country.

Such reports of what was happening in Ethiopia were also being received from many other countries, swelling the files of records kept in the offices in Los Angeles. While Christian radio broadcasts were reaching more and more people in the major languages, Gospel Recordings was going beyond those frontiers to people and areas in geographical or cultural isolation. To reach these smaller, less accessible groups was still Joy's over-riding desire, and it kept her on the move, speaking on their behalf when she was not actually travelling among them. She was often far away from Los Angeles, and since long-distance telephone calls are very expensive, even in off-peak hours, she came to the point quickly when decisions had to be made or advice given.

'Follow the Jericho pattern for the remaining seven days,' were her laconic instructions when she learned that only half the amount required to meet the purchase deadline on urgently needed property was in hand. She was phoning from Wheaton, Illinois. The property in question, ideally suited for head-quarter offices and storage departments, was situated in the same block as the Gospel Recordings factory, and only three minutes' walk from the over-crowded compound in Witmer Street. A deposit of $6,000 had been paid in September on the understanding that it would be forfeited if the balance were not forthcoming in October. So convinced had both Board and

staff been that God intended them to have that property for
which they had prayed for months, that when the opportunity
came they took it and paid the deposit. Now the deadline had
been brought forward three days, and with only a week to go
the money in hand was less than $30,000. Twice that amount
was needed.

'Follow the Jericho pattern!' said Joy. 'And cable the
Branch offices to join us.' No-one else was to be told of the
situation. It was between Gospel Recordings and God alone.

The staff at Los Angeles understood. The walls of Jericho
had fallen after the Israelites had encircled the city each day
for seven days, and the analogy was clear. 'Our march was a
two-hour cessation from our labours each day, when our entire
staff met from 2 p.m. to 4 p.m. to encircle the wall by prayer,
song, confession, forgiveness, praise. Signals were flashed to
Australia – London – Cape Town – India – Canada:
BUILDING DEADLINE OCTOBER NINTH FOLLOW
JERICHO PATTERN NEXT SEVEN DAYS JOSHUA 3.5.'

Joy was on a speaking tour, but she kept the vigil too, and
on the fourth day she was deeply impressed by the words in
the first chapter of the book of Joshua, 'Within three days ye
shall pass over this Jordan to go in to possess the land . . .' At
the same time the staff in Los Angeles, unknown to her, were
conscious of an emphasis on the same verse. But no money
had come in. The coffers were empty.

The following afternoon the telephone bell rang in the Los
Angeles office. It was an overseas call, from London,
England. David Chapman, newly appointed secretary of the
British branch was speaking. 'A legacy has just been received
– the Council feels it must be meant for you – a few other
gifts have come in, too – all being transferred to your
banking account . . .' He mentioned the sum. It was sufficient
to cover the balance required to complete the purchase of the
property.

The walls of Jericho had fallen – two days ahead of time!
When the staff at Los Angeles recovered from their surprise at
the source of God's supply and the accuracy of it, they burst
into a spontaneous doxology. Joy continued her speaking tour

with further evidence to produce that God is alive today and worthy, oh, so worthy, to be praised!

She had many encouraging things to report in those years of the early 1960s. Gospel Recordings achievements of obtaining new languages had soared again as the prayer for more recordists was answered. The end of the previous decade had seen a dramatic drop in the addition of languages, though there had been a substantial increase in the number of records distributed. During the years when the three recording teams had been on the field – the Trio, Vaughn Collins and Don Richter – the total figure of new languages had risen to 1,837. At one time it was reported that the studio in Los Angeles was receiving fresh recordings that had been done at the rate of one every two days. With the return on leave of the full-time recordists, however, the figure dropped steeply, although 166 in two years were added by part-time workers. Now the figure was rising again. Teams of recordists were out on the field – Vaughn Collins and Ted Jones in South America, Don Richter and his wife in New Guinea, Ann Sherwood and Kathy Hoffmeyer in Africa, Noela Elvery and Evelyn Baillie in Asia, Daniel Grossenbacher and John Rothgerber 'the two Swiss boys' somewhere in the Sahara, Jill Bembrick and Nell Gibson in India . . .

When Gospel Recordings celebrated its 25th anniversary in 1964 Joy was able to announce that the simple Gospel of Jesus Christ had been proclaimed in 3,109 languages and dialects, reaching hundreds of thousands of people who had never heard it before, and who could hear it in no other way than by means of the little records.

The records! The whirling discs with the captured voices that proclaimed Jesus as the victor over sin, evil spirits, death!

The listening groups of naked, primitive people here, the isolated nomads there, the by-passed clusters of illiterates in the urban districts, the hamlets and villages off the beaten tracks . . . !

The wonder of it never ceased to inspire her, this means that God had put into her hands of reaching everyone in his own tongue to tell what Jesus could do for his soul. 'Ask God to bless the records,' she urged her listeners. 'Every time you ask Him to bless the food you eat, ask Him also to bless the records.' Of themselves, those records were but dead things. Only as God infused the words with spiritual power could they be true messengers of life — and God worked in answer to prayer and praise, not in answer to mere interest.

The following year was a particularly exhausting yet colourful one for her. She went to Arizona in the hottest time of the year to make recordings and help train a team of young women. Then she set out on a trip that was to take her eventually to a country no Gospel Recordings field recordist had ever succeeded in entering — Colombia. Harrowing tales of the persecution of Christians there had been coming out for years, but now there seemed a slight easing of the situation, and Joy was determined to get in if she could. Her companion was young Jim Mittelstedt, and they were to be joined by Mrs. Charlotte Marcy, an experienced member of the Central America Mission.

Their journey took them down through Mexico, Guatemala, El Salvador, Honduras, Nicaragua, Costa Rica and Panama. Her letters back to Los Angeles reported going off the beaten tracks in several of those countries, including an exciting adventure of pursuing a tribe up the Bayano River in Panama to record in a section of the Cuna tribe. She made light of the attendant discomforts and dangers of such trips — the important thing was to find the necessary informers and interpreters who could act as links in passing on those heavenly messages, sentence by sentence, till the tribesman was speaking them in his own tongue and his own idiom, telling out clearly something that was news to him as it would be to the other members of his community when eventually they had the phonette and records in their own hands. A new message could easily enter the gate of the ear on a friendly intelligible voice.

On their way through Honduras they visited Marcala again. They arrived when a conference was in progress and, 'It was just great to be there! The chapel was filled and looked so nice. Many of them were my children in the Lord, or their children by either natural or spiritual birth. I had a little opportunity to speak to the congregation — everybody was happy and full of joy.

'On Sunday morning I felt I should go to a little town on the border. It is way back in the mountains on a road that got worse and worse. We left about 7 a.m. and arrived about 10.30 a.m., but the time of fellowship was worth the rugged driving and hiking. I met a man who had been converted in prison one Christmas day when I went with some of the believers to preach and take gifts. He had been truly saved and returned to his village to witness. Now there are other believers and a little chapel which they have built with their own hands.'

Back to Marcala in time for the evening service, the chapel crowded to the doors. 'Souls were saved . . . Once again I was able to plead with them to come to the feet of the Lord Jesus. I also had a great time of prayer with Don Pedro who had been with me all those years in Marcala. What a man of prayer he is! What an inspiration to know he will be following us in prayer!'

On to the capital city, where she met some of the men who as lads had been in her three-month Bible School in Marcala. 'Some of them are the main preachers of the country today, and it thrilled my heart to have a time to pray on our knees together. I cannot tell you the joy there has been seeing my children walking with the Lord.' Even news of the success of the records could not supersede such delight. It was the fulfilment of her highest desires for the people of Marcala.

Enjoyment of another type awaited her as she travelled on. For years she had looked forward to an opportunity to travel through the Panama Canal, and now she was to experience it. She rose very early in the morning to watch the process, and saw in it a spiritual truth she could not keep to herself. The only way for the boat to reach its destination was to steam slowly into the imprisonment of the lock, then turn off its engine. Shut in from behind, oppressed by the height of the water in the next lock, there was nothing to do but wait. 'To try to help the situation by turning on its motor could have wrecked the ship as well as destroy the lock.' Slowly the vessel was lifted as the waters were poured in, and when the right height was reached the gates were opened, and the ship sailed through.

'How much this is like our spiritual life. God prepares us and lets us wait until His time is ready. Then He lifts us up, opens the gates, and moves us on.'

As they drew near to Colombia they encountered what looked like being an insuperable obstacle. They would not be allowed to take their car into the country, they were informed, unless they left a deposit of two thousand American dollars in the bank. The arrangement must be made through the A.A.A. in New York.

Two thousand American dollars! They did not possess that amount of money. They had been planning to travel widely during the three months they expected to spend in Colombia, for Joy wanted to study the situation thoroughly, to discover all the missionary work being done, either in Spanish or in Indian dialects, as well as start recording. Without the car to travel in, and store the various things necessary for their enterprise, they could not accomplish a quarter of what they had planned.

Two thousand American dollars! 'I'll phone Virginia, and see if there is any money on my account,' said Joy, not very expectantly. Gifts were frequently received ear-marked for her personal use, but they were usually comparatively small. However, she put through the long-distance call, and heard Virginia Miller's voice at the other end of the line.

'Oh, Joy, I'm glad to hear from you,' she said. 'I didn't know how to contact you. We've just received two thousand pounds sterling for you from England. I've never heard of the donor. Yes, it's a personal gift for you. I know! You've never had anything like it before, but its yours all right! Oh! Oh, all right. I'll see the right amount is lodged in the bank in New York . . . !'

It was one of those occasions when it was not difficult to rejoice whole-heartedly. The apparently insurmountable obstacle had not actually existed at all, since the money was already in hand – a larger sum than Joy had ever received, and from a totally unexpected source.

The next step was not so easy. The car must remain in customs until the necessary papers were received, and that might take as long as a month. Meanwhile, they had arrived in the Colombian port, and must find somewhere to stay. There appeared to be no taxis for hire, and a noisy altercation on the wharf ended up rather ignominiously with the three of them walking behind a little cart on which was piled all their luggage, looking for a hotel.

'It didn't take us long to realise that even according to Buenaventura standards we had picked a low-rate one,' wrote Joy later. 'In a hot place this was hotter, in a dirty city this was dirtier, and in a place with few modern conveniences this had the fewest ... Some of our rejoicing was more by faith than by sight!'

They looked round the dark, windowless room that had been allotted them, tried to brush off the flies that settled on their faces, wondered how they would ever be able to eat anything in this filthy place, and whether the D.D.T. they had brought would be sufficient to deal with the fleas and the lice.

Then the people started coming in. They wanted to look at Americans at close range. The only tourists they were accustomed to seeing sped off in luxurious cars and disappeared quickly into expensive hotels. It was as good as a fiesta to have Americans right here where anyone could go in and have a look at them!

Their coming transformed the situation for Joy, at any rate. If she was as good as a fiesta, they were as good as a congregation! They spoke Spanish, of course, and she promptly produced a Phonette and put on a record Vaughn Collins had recently made in Argentina. The singing in it sounded especially sweet and clear, and in the dirty, over-crowded room the words rang out,

> 'Come into my heart, Lord Jesus,
> There is room in my heart for Thee ...'

They listened entranced to the singing, though most of them lost interest when the message that followed it began to dig deep into their consciences. There was one, however, whose heart was touched right from the start. Twenty-one year old Rosalba, mother of a very restless baby, had never heard anything like it before. She had heard about Jesus being born in a manger and crucified on a cross, but she knew nothing about Him being alive today. After hovering around the *Americanas'* stuffy hotel room for two or three days, she eventually had the opportunity for the talk she longed for. She wanted to know more about the Way, she told Joy.

'Charlotte took the baby so that I could give undivided attention to explaining to her in her own language how very simple and beautiful it was to invite Jesus Christ into her heart. We closed the door of the little cell-like room and knelt on the hard floor beside the bed with wooden slats instead of springs, and there she really did ask the Saviour to come in.'

There was no doubt about the reality of Rosalba's conversion. She was quite sure the Lord Jesus had come into her heart, and she wanted the man she was living with, father of her baby, to ask Him in, too. Don Luciano was quite prepared to be friendly when Jim Mittelstedt talked to him, and said he thought this Gospel way was good, but he wasn't ready to go along – not yet. The only thing that made it hard to leave that port, and the most unpleasant accommodation Joy had ever known, was saying goodbye to Rosalba. 'We'll go on praying for you, and for Don Luciano,' Joy assured her. 'God will hear our prayers . .' But she did not really expect to meet Rosalba again.

It was as well that they had got in touch with Christian and Missionary Alliance missionaries in the city of Cali, and been assured there was plenty of room for them there in the guest house. 'Come as quickly as you can – don't dilly dally in that awful port – it's got a bad name!' Joy's weakened constitution could not have stood out much longer against the unusually unhygienic conditions in the third-rate port hotel. When they eventually arrived after a long ride through the mountains, and made their way to the clean, spacious guest house, she was already beginning to feel ill, and succumbed thankfully to the luxury of a room to herself again, and the privacy of wholesome bathrooms that smelt fresh and with doors that could be locked.

'There is also a laundry with washing machine and the house has conveniences of every kind, even to a pop-up toaster,' she reported light-heartedly. Joy appreciated the good things of this life when they were available, and the daily thanksgivings with which she concluded each day often made reference to the nice things she had had to eat. She had no complaints to make about being feverish, and feeling nauseated, and having unpleasant evidences that although all was well with her soul, the same could not be said for her body.

'My feet have been kept off the ground for the last ten days or so because of a vicious Colombian bug that has attached himself to me along with his relatives. But we are still having fun and incidentally getting a lot of necessary things done in preparation for our tour.' The preparations included writing letters, introducing themselves, to 200 missionaries in Colombia.

It was rather surprising, therefore, that two days before Christmas, when she was feeling better and was busy at her desk, she should suddenly yield to an impulse to go shopping. It seemed unreasonable, and not really necessary, but – 'Let's go to town right away,' she said to Charlotte. She met with no resistance there. Charlotte was always ready for anything, especially excitement, so off they went. They travelled by bus, since that only cost two cents whereas a taxi cost eighteen, and arriving in the crowded city, brilliantly and attractively decorated for the festive season, they made their way to a huge Colombian equivalent of an inexpensive supermarket. They would buy a few little oddments as presents for their Spanish neighbours, they decided, 'and one or two little things to wrap up for each other to sort of pretend we're at home.'

As they were struggling through the mob of shoppers, surrounded by a galaxy of faces, one face drew close to Joy with an expression of astonished delight.

'Senorita Joy!'

'Rosalba!' Joy and Charlotte exclaimed incredulously, then embraced her ecstatically. They had expected never to see her again yet here she was, their spiritual babe, eagerly greeting them in a city of 400,000 people, and more than one hundred miles away from where they had said goodbye. 'And Don Luciano! Here!' Rosalba's family lived in Cali, and she had come to stay with them, Don Luciano accompanying her.

Joy and Charlotte knew now why they had been impelled to embark on what seemed a totally unnecessary excursion.

A week later Joy was ill in bed again, so Charlotte and Jim set off to visit Rosalba's family. When they returned, very late, Charlotte's face was aglow.

'Did you have a good time?' asked Joy eagerly.

'Guess what happened,' said Charlotte.

Joy hesitated. Then she said, 'Did Don Luciano accept the Lord?' It seemed too much to expect, though it was what they had prayed for.

'Yes!' said Charlotte. She was so excited she could scarcely speak. 'And so did Rosalba's mother – and so did her sisters – and so did her only brother. The only one who didn't was her father, and he was drunk!'

When they recovered somewhat from their jubilation and had time to reflect, they had no difficulty in agreeing that all things had worked together for good – delays and filthy hotels included. And as Joy pointed out, it had all started with a little record in Spanish. They could not have asked for a more propitious entry into the country.

Joy had made no more than very rough plans for the months in Colombia. Experiences in previous recording trips had proved that it was a Guide rather than a blue-print that was needed. Unexpected delays, illness, breakdowns in communications all militated against a tight schedule, and her practice of rejoicing in them all not only preserved her and her companions in travel from anxiety and frustration, but kept them alert to grasp the opportunity that had been ripening in secret, and which might have been missed if they had been unwatchful. When, therefore, Charlotte Marcy said she felt she should go to Costa Rica to attend the 75th Anniversary

Conference of her mission, and it was found the only way to get there was by plane from Medellin, to Medellin they went. Joy had not planned to go there, and it involved driving through the night over bandit-ridden mountains to do so, but they arrived in time to see Charlotte off 'gaily dressed in a new pleated skirt and a pongee blouse she had bought in Panama. She looked right smart.'

Now it so happened that, unknown to Joy, a conference of missionaries was being held in the Oriental Missionary Society's centre at Medellin. She could not have arrived at a better time for meeting the very people she wanted to get in touch with. Many of them were using records that had been made by Vaughn Collins in other countries of South America, and sent in to Colombia. They were encouraging in the advice they gave.

'The time is ripe!'

'The way is open as never before.'

'Everything is converging – this is the time of opportunity to reach the Indian tribes.'

At the large Saturday evening meeting of the conference one missionary, reporting on her work, showed slides in which the central feature was the phonette and the records. This was the only way she could preach to the Cuna people, she said, for she did not know their language.

'It was as effective a presentation of G.R. as could be,' wrote Joy enthusiastically. 'People want the records and God has made wonderful preparation for us here in Colombia. The country has gone daffy over records, and multitudes have electric players ... There is need for the records among all classes. Eighty per cent are illiterate; just meditate on that. They are nice looking, nicely dressed, cultured and civilised people. One would expect them to be literate, yet they are in great need, and in addition to these there are multitudes of Indians.'

They travelled widely in the following weeks, their journeys taking them up through Guajira Indian country in the northern deserts of Colombia and into Venezuela. Charlotte had rejoined them and one Saturday night, after dealing with two punctured tyres, they arrived at the city of Caracas. To their dismay the city looked worse than New York or Philadelphia for driving in, with traffic that seemed to thread in and out of a maze at an alarming pace. They had made no arrangements to stay anywhere, they did not know their way about, and they were very hungry.

'Lord, show us a restaurant,' they prayed urgently as they parked by the side of the road. They knew they couldn't stop for more than a minute. 'Show us where we can park the car, how to get around this block, how to drive down these streets.' Then they moved on again. In a short time they found themselves outside a Chinese restaurant, with parking space beside it. 'Thank you, Lord,' Joy breathed, then said,

'You two go in and order dinner, while I put through a phone call.'

She had developed a habit of collecting names and telephone numbers, and she had one, just one, in the city of Caracas. A Southern Baptist missionary, by the name of Clark. She did not know him, but dialled the number, and to her relief heard a man's voice with the welcome drawl of the southern states. 'Mr. Clark . . . ?' She explained who she was, and wondered if he could recommend anywhere for her and her two companions to spend the night.

'I'll come and get you,' he said cheerfully. 'But I can't get there till twelve midnight. Just wait around till I come.' So early on Sunday morning they found themselves crawling contentedly into freshly made beds with the prayer that as they had only two days in which to pack the sort of enquiries and interviews that would normally take a month, they would be enabled to manage it somehow.

Once more they found they had arrived at the right place at the right time. Not only were they able to learn what they wanted to know about the missionary situation in Venezuela and the prospects for recording among the remoter tribes, but they were brought in touch with a man who enthusiastically offered his help.

'Yes, I will receive freight shipments at the port and re-ship them to points in the country.

'I'll take you to the Chief of Customs. We know him, and he is very favourable these days. But the political complexion is not good,' she was warned. 'The time is short.' So although her purpose in going to Venezuela had been primarily to survey the situation and merely pave the way for recording teams to go in later on, Jim sat down and made some recordings then and there.

'The experiences of the past days almost make us breathless,' she wrote a short time later, when they were back in Colombia. They had stayed at eleven different towns in three weeks, arriving unannounced in most cases and not knowing where to go, but in each case they had been directed to a place where there were missionaries who welcomed them. True, they had not always been able to reach a town in time to spend the night there. In one place, having transferred all their belongings to canoes, they had to stay in a *finca*, a tropical farm, and were delayed there an extra day. 'We were not disappointed as we had left it in the Lord's hands. We were thrilled to be out among these people of a different type and to witness to them.' Joy found her way to the kitchen, and started talking to the little group lounging there.

'I couldn't believe in the Lord,' said one woman after listening for a little time. 'I can't read,' she added in explanation.

'The Lord didn't say it was through reading,' retorted Joy promptly. 'He said faith comes by hearing! Now you listen to these records ...' The outcome of that kitchen meeting was that the woman heard and believed. 'She was full of joy and began to witness to it right away.'

They travelled for hours through territory that was inhabited by Indians, among whom was not one missionary or Christian Colombian to tell them of Christ in their own dialects. 'Praise God, we have records!' wrote Joy. 'Remember there are over 100 tribes in Colombia alone. Stand by and pray for our team as they prepare to return next year. These things are only accomplished by prayer and faith.'

The four months' trip concluded in Ecuador, where by means of an amateur radio operator in California Joy had a chat with the staff in Los Angeles. All three of them were well, she reported. Jim and Charlotte expected to travel home by boat. A petition for importation and duty exemption on 10,000 records and 200 Phonettes for Colombia was going to the customs authorities there for approval.

As for her, she would be returning for one day in Colombia before flying to Florida for a brief visit with Anthony and Sanna Rossi. Then she was going on to the World Congress of Missions in Wheaton, Illinois. No, she wouldn't be home in Los Angeles for some time yet.

*   *   *

About this time a change took place in the policy of Gospel Recordings regarding field recordists. It was decided that the five-year restriction on engagement and marriage should be reduced to four years.

When Jim Mittelstedt heard the news, he put through a long distance phone call. He had not been in touch with the girl friend he had made a complete break with four years ago after talking to Joy at the airport, when he had known so surely that that was the best thing to do. He had never doubted the wisdom of the decision. But now the test was over. He wondered if she would remember him at all, whether she was married to someone else. He'd like to find out.

Yes, she was still single. Yes, she was willing to see him. Jim bought a plane ticket . . .

11

Rainbow in the Clouds

No LIFE-STORY OF Joy Ridderhof, however superficial, would be complete without reference to the period spanning the years 1966 to 1968. Outwardly, as far as her activities were concerned, there was little about it to distinguish it from others. Her travels at home and abroad continued, and she spoke at numerous meetings, maintained a voluminous correspondence. The end of 1966 found her travelling by car in Europe, the staccato notes made in her little pocket diary giving the sketchiest idea of what was actually contained in her days.

27.12.66 Car key hole blocked. To Amsterdam. Lunch in car. Hunting for hotel. Supper Wimpeys.

28.12.66 Shopping in Amsterdam. Visited girls on Bible Club boat.

30.12.66 Spoke at Ede.

31.12.66 Returned from Ede. Raining. Good to get home. Prayer.

She went on to the little town of Halver where Ann Sherwood with Marlene Muhr from France were establishing the first Gospel Recordings base in Europe.

1.1.67 Halver. We had a virus in our system. Ann dizzy. Good day prayer. Blessed fellowship.

2.1.67 Stayed in to write letters.

    3.1.67 Wonderful promise about eagles wings . . .
    4.1.67 Kindness of young people on train.
    5.1.67 Train trip to Brake.
    6.1.67 My cold gone! Important mail sent off.

The following week she was travelling in Switzerland —
Basel — Le Locle — Lausanne. On arrival in Geneva she noted
briefly in her diary that she had a headache, and reminded
herself of things to do.

    18.1.67 Write to Marjorie about clothes. Sanna about fruit
             cake. M.C. about other answers. Ánn about
             money. Cassette to Board. David as to my arrival
             in Bombay.

Before the end of the month she was in India, then she went
on to Australia and New Zealand. The following year she went
to India again.

The work in the various centres, Australia, England, India,
South Africa, Europe was prospering, and it was during this
period that the Gospel Recordings centre in Canada was
officially opened with John Gray in charge. He and his wife
had returned from Bangalore to look after his elderly mother,
their earthly possessions contained in two suitcases and two
45-gallon drums. In a very short time they had found
themselves in possession of a furnished house with ten rooms,
and almost simultaneously had received an invitation from
Gospel Recordings in Los Angeles to set up a distribution
centre in Toronto.

Gospel Recordings as an international organisation was
evidently forging ahead.

But Joy knew that at the very heart of it, in Los Angeles
itself, there was uneasiness. Just as years before, on the outset
of the memorable first overseas recording trip to the Philippines a pall seemed to have descended on the team working
there, so it was now, though with a subtle difference. Previously there had been no threat to Joy's leadership. If her
administrative methods were acknowledged as being some-

what haphazard, no-one had doubted that her vision, her faith and her intimate knowledge of every aspect of the work qualified her to be Director of the organisation she had brought into being. But now that was being questioned. Even the Board, with its final authority, was uncertain about it until a sudden turn of events settled the matter and established her position. But during that stormy period nine workers, for various reasons, resigned. They included — the head of the stamper department and his assistant; the two deputation speakers; the executive secretary; the lathe operator; the two in charge of the press room.

Although the field recordists were largely unaffected by what happened in Los Angeles, it was during this same period that several of them left the work. Vaughn Collins was the first, and Joy could scarcely believe it. Vaughn who had never complained, who had endured hardships of which he made no mention and of which she only heard from others; who, when asked once how he did it, what made him press on alone, steeling himself against the softer things of life, had answered quietly, 'The Judgment!' It didn't seem possible that God was calling him now into another type of missionary work, in which Gospel Recordings could have only a secondary claim on him. She rejoiced on principle, but it was a long time before she could really accept it.

Then there was Kathleen Hoffmeyer. Kathy had heard about G.R. from Vaughn Collins and Don Richter when she was a student at Prairie Bible College, and as a result had gone to Los Angeles as an I.C.L. She wanted to be a recordist but said nothing about it except to the Lord, and one day Joy had asked, 'Would you be willing to go to Nigeria? Ann Sherwood is there now and needs a fellow worker.' Kathy had dissolved into tears of joy, and although she was short of U.S. $40 to pay the fare for her flight the day before she was due to leave, she received it in time, and other gifts sufficient for her to take U.S. $200 in travellers cheques with her.

She'd had her exciting experiences in Nigeria, too. She was not supposed to travel alone, but she did so sometimes anyhow, and on one occasion her car broke down three times in country where she'd been warned not to stop even if she knocked someone down! 'Go on to the next police point and report it, but don't stop till you get there!' she'd been told. She hadn't stopped, but the car had, and now what was she to do? A man on a bicycle came along and got it started again the first time. The second time the car stopped it was some African war dancers with white painted faces who cheerfully managed it for her. The third time it was a Roman Catholic priest in his chauffeur-driven car who came to her rescue. She was a good recordist too was Kathy, and always came up smiling. It wasn't surprising that when Colin met her in Kenya he wanted to marry her, and Joy had no great difficulty about rejoicing over that. She didn't expect girl recordists to remain single all their lives, and Kathy had helped capture over one hundred voices during her stay in Africa.

But it meant that another recordist was off the field.

It was the same with Evelyn Baillie. For five years she'd been a field recordist in the Philippines, then in Africa, with over sixty new languages wrested in some cases out of as grim and discouraging experiences as Joy herself had ever known. It hadn't been easy for the young American to team up with an Australian whom she had never met before, and head off on a trip in the Philippines which included plunging into a head-hunting tribe that had taken their last head two weeks earlier. It was on that trip trudging through the jungle with their packs, including the Nagra, on their backs that Noela Elvery, the Australian, had complained to the Lord, 'Where are the men? This isn't women's work – I'm a soft city girl, I go everywhere in cars. I can't take it.' The answer she received had fortified her for all that lay ahead. '*To you, as a woman, I have given the privilege of introducing the Gospel to these people.*' Evelyn had shared in that, and when, in 1967, she married George Janzen of the Los Angeles staff, Joy rejoiced. Evelyn had done a good job on the field. There would be those among the multitude before the Throne who would be there only because Evelyn had responded when God called her.

But who would take her place?

Then there were 'the two Swiss boys', Dan Grossenbacher

and Jean-Jacques Rothgerber. Since 1963 they had been going
on recording trips into Africa's remotest spots, capturing 275
languages in the four years. But now the time had come, as Joy
had known it must, that they would enter into the work for
which they had been preparing. They'd do what they could in
the future when opportunity arose, to capture more languages,
but now they must move on.

Ted Jones, too. He joined Wycliffe Bible Translators, and
that was something to praise God for. But it meant one less
G.R. recordist.

Then, in 1969, Don and Eunice Richter resigned. Between
them they had captured over 300 languages, some among very
fierce tribes in New Guinea, and there had been some
remarkable conversions. Don had been at it for nearly twenty
years – but now he believed God was calling in another
direction, and it meant leaving Gospel Recordings.

Those were shadowed years. Joy's resilient spirit and deep-
seated confidence that God would work it all out for good
helped her to stand up to the reverses. Her manner of life, too,
as she continued to travel widely, made ever changing and
immediate demands on her which in measure off-set the grief
she felt as one after another resigned from the work. For the
depleted teams in the factory, the studio and the offices in Los
Angeles it was different. They were there all the time, and at
one period Virginia Miller found herself almost dreading the
weekly prayer days, coming to them with the lurking fear,
'Whose resignation will be announced this time?' On them,
too, fell the burden of maintaining the work, fulfilling the
orders for records that continued to flood in, dealing with
problems that arose to which no one seemed to have the right
answer. Worst of all, perhaps, were the murmurs that reached
them of what was being said, 'The glory has departed from
Gospel Recordings.' Too busy now to maintain the flow of
information that sustained the interest of supporters, too busy
to respond to invitations from churches to 'come and speak
about the work', it was all they could do to keep the work itself
going.

But God who giveth songs in the night, had inner joys for

them about which those outside knew nothing. The sense of unity among them deepened to new levels, and the original team, Virginia, Doris, Al Rethey, the Dyks, the Olsons, Mable Erlandson, were reminded of the early days when together they had joyfully shouldered the burdens of the exciting new organisation. Also, the flow of letters from all parts of the world, reporting on the results from the records, continued unabated. Whatever was happening at Los Angeles wasn't stopping the little discs from whirling, sounding out in voices the listeners could understand the fact that Jesus died and came to life again, opening the door of everlasting life to all mankind. That news was still the power of God unto salvation to everyone that believed, and as far as they were concerned there was nothing to compare with proclaiming it, even if it did mean longer hours than ever in the factory, filling in forms for the export authorities, completing the hundred and one tasks that needed to be done. While they were busy about those practical details from morning till into the night in Los Angeles, God was working salvation in the midst of the earth, and it wasn't difficult to rejoice over that!

Furthermore, they had the comforting evidence that their Master was with them in the very practical matter of financial supplies. Gospel Recordings never accumulated any capital, and rarely had substantial reserves on which to draw. The money that was given was spent on the work. Over the years there had been times when funds were low, when economies were stringently practised, when the staff had been called privately for prayer that the money urgently needed would be forthcoming. But during the dark period when general outside interest was subsiding, when Gospel Recordings was given no publicity, when there were even those who assumed it was closing down, at the very time when income might have been expected to subside the funds flowed in so smoothly, so lavishly, that there was never any need to think about money except to give thanks for it. The Lord who tempers every storm, and knows how much His servants can bear, saw to it that no financial embarrassments were added to their trials. Among other unexpected provisions a number of legacies fell due just at that time.

There was another thing that bound them together which had nothing whatever to do with the work. It was a simple but very deep human sorrow. Stephen Brown's parents had known about Joy before she went to Honduras, and later, as missionaries themselves in Guatemala, used the records frequently, were convinced of their value, and after returning to Los Angeles joined Gospel Recordings. Stephen, therefore, was known to all, since Joy insisted that Gospel Recordings workers' children were all members of the family, and when the lad fell ill there was general concern. Throughout the whole of the darkest period in Gospel Recordings history his parents had the added grief of knowing their only child was in constant pain. His complaint was eventually diagnosed as incurable. In 1971 he died. The sympathy and tenderness which this pain and sorrow in their midst drew out from all of the team threaded indefinably into the fabric of life, knitting them together, adding a quality of gentle affection to their comradeship. Sorrow and pain have strange and enriching uses.

The admiration of those remaining on the staff for Joy deepened during this period. The work which meant more to her than life itself was obviously being tested to an unusual degree, yet in spite of it – perhaps because of it – her spirit of rejoicing soared. She sincerely believed God was over all, and that out of the trials He would bring triumphs. They knew her faith was genuine, and their own faith was strengthened by it, while her love for them was quickened by their loyalty. When she was away on her long and sometimes erratic travels she wrote to them frequently, long and chatty letters in which she quite unconsciously paid tribute to the many people whom God had sent to help her. However defective her memory might be for other matters, it was prodigious when it came to colleagues and friends. In one long letter she wrote to 'Dear, dear family,' she mentioned over fifty people by name, with something about each one that revealed an intimate knowledge of their affairs.

In 1968 she started off on a journey that was to take her round the world, and she was ill at the time of leaving.

'What a pleasure it is to travel with the Lord Jesus as Companion and Guide,' she wrote from India, relating her experiences en route. 'Yes, it is even fun, because He carries all the burdens.' Then she went on to enumerate some of the ways in which He did it.

A lady in Denver vacated the best rooms of her home so that Joy could be alone there with Ann, who had arranged to meet her.

'Ann arrived when I was at the lowest rung physically. Without her assistance I would not have been able to get through my meetings.'

She was suffering acutely from bursitis. 'At the right time the Lord sent me to . . . a consecrated Christian doctor . . . The pain began to ebb and within ten days had almost ceased, and now it is completely gone.'

She arrived in London extremely tired, and to her delight was met by the Livingston Hoggs. 'Muriel has been my comfort and support many times when in physical need, and this time she had a bed ready and literally tucked me in. It was my precious Companion and Prince doing this through her.'

The list of addresses of people she could contact in Europe that was posted to her from Los Angeles did not arrive in time. 'But my Guide did not need the information. In Holland I was met by our worker, Marlene Muhr, who was right on deck in Amsterdam.

'What a blessing it was to see her and to deposit all my "too much" luggage and let her take over, to drive, to find places, and I am ashamed to say, to pay the bills as well. She felt the Lord had sent her some extra provisions for this very purpose, and we had a wonderful time. Although I wasn't too well my Elder Brother gave strength and gladness for all that was needed.' They travelled in Holland, West Germany and Switzerland, then she set off for Turkey and Israel.

'I arrived in Istanbul, on a very late flight from Barcelona. Everything was so strange on arrival. How should I get money changed? How much should I pay the porter? Where should I stay? Somehow I latched on to an Indian businessman and his wife and did what they did ...' She shared a taxi with them and 'just relaxed knowing that there would be a resting place soon. Then the taxi stopped at the great glamorous Hilton Hotel!'

It wasn't what she expected, or what she would have chosen, and when she found herself being assigned a private room with bath she did not know what to do. But, 'Sometimes my Elder Brother, who is also a Prince, likes to treat His family to the best, so I did not fuss.' Instead, she enjoyed a delicious bath and the benefits of modern comforts, and later, in the spacious lounge, 'I had the opportunity to witness to a hungry-hearted South African lady who was travelling alone.'

A telephone call to the only Istanbul number she had in her book seemed rather unlikely to elicit any useful response, since she knew no Turkish. But there was a phone in her room, so she decided to try, and to her amazement an English voice answered. 'My "host" on the phone saw that I was entertained in two Turkish homes and given a personally conducted tour of the city. Some meetings were soon arranged in two different churches. This visit, arranged I am sure by my Elder Brother, opened up exciting new vistas for Gospel Recordings Ministry.' This was always her primary consideration. What possibilities were there for the distribution of records, where were there people with no Word of God in their own language, were there any ethnic groups among whom a voice could be captured ... ? There were great barriers as well as great needs in Turkey, she discovered. One visit there did more to enlighten her than a dozen letters.

In Israel she met an old friend who 'couldn't have done more for me if I had been a queen. The Israel experience was thrilling — a great privilege. There are untapped opportunities for greater distribution there but the high tax or duty is almost prohibitive.'

'All this time my Elder Brother and I were headed for India,' she continued. David Macnaughtan was to be married in Poona, but there was no scheduled flight due to arrive there in time. 'However, I felt certain my Prince wanted me to go to the wedding.' So she made enquiries, and decided the next step should be a midnight flight to Pakistan. 'It was a packed plane. I am sure my Guide wanted me in it, because I was able to witness to a Pakistani surgeon en route.'

So she arrived, unheralded, in Karachi. The first thing to do was to book a flight for Bombay, from where she could get to Poona by train. Having done that her mind flew to her permanent business – Gospel Recordings. There was time to meet their distributor in Karachi, if only she knew where to find him. But in this unknown city of millions of people, how could she locate him?

As always, her question took the form of prayer, swift, spontaneous, conversational. Just as simply the answer was given.

The name of Bishop Chandu Ray came to mind. Perhaps he could help her. She had heard that he was to be in Singapore about that time, attending an important conference, but decided nevertheless to look for his address in the telephone book. 'I feel hopeless looking up telephone numbers in foreign phone books, but I did find it ...' She somehow had the conviction that this would be a lead, so instead of phoning hired a taxi which took her direct to the church office, several miles away.

'And there he was, Chandu Ray himself. After a chat and a cup of tea he phoned a friend thinking he might know how to locate our distributor, Marlin Summers ... A short time later Marlin Summers arrived at the church and carried Joy off to meet his wife and children. 'How wonderful to have a Brother-Companion-Guide who can make a way when there is no way!'

On she went to Bombay – and thence to Poona by train.

'The train pulled into Poona. I did not know where to find David Macnaughtan or the wedding party, but there, wreathed in smiles and looking straight at me through the window of the train was David, the groom. What a happy occasion that was. We of Gospel Recordings are so grateful to God for this lovely new worker, Alice Byers, now Mrs. David Macnaughtan.'

Joy was invited to visit the Ramabai Mukti Mission, and

arrived so exhausted and feverish she had to go straight to bed.

'The Lord had it all arranged. They gave me the nicest room and put a girl at my service to bring breakfast or tea and snacks and to keep me supplied with everything I needed. The Lord knew there was a hospital there and a dear Australian nurse to look in on me each day. I am thrilled to see what He has prepared,' she concluded, 'and look forward to the remainder of my journey with Him.'

That particular journey took her on to Africa – Ethiopia, Sudan, Kenya, Tanzania, Malawi, Rhodesia, Mozambique, Congo, Nigeria, Ghana, Ivory Coast, Liberia, Sierra Leone, Guinea, Gambia, Senegal, South Africa. After that she took a plane to Brazil . . .

A year later she was in Colombia again, to attend a Latin American Congress with over 900 delegates before going on to South America and then to the West Indies.

'What a surprise and blessing it was to learn a day after my arrival here that our own Larry DeVilbiss had come in from his work in Panama.' Larry DeVilbiss had come to Gospel Recordings in 1965 and was now one of its most experienced and daring field recordists. His journeys took him deep into the jungles. Travelling at times with little more than his recording machine he had learned to live off the land, existing for days on end on what he could find in the forests. He was reluctant to talk of his experiences which, when reporters heard of them, sent them eagerly on his track. To have him with her on this occasion was an encouragement, for she always drew strength from the companionship of members of her own G.R. family. Together they introduced the records to those who knew nothing about them, handing out 1,000 individually to people who returned to nearly every corner of Latin America.

The Congress over, they went their separate ways again.

'Larry will be heading out to the tribes immediately,' she reported. 'He has a lead through a government officer to go to one of the most ferocious tribes of South America. One tribe of 2,000 possesses a huge area of land in Colombia and Venezuela. After praying for this tribe for twenty years, could this be the time when we will be able to get messages recorded for them that will give them the essence of the message we have known for so long?'

Give them the essence of the message we have known for so long. This was her consuming desire, and it kept her on the move.

. . . To Latin America.

. . . To Texas.

. . . To Canada.

. . . To Colombia.

. . . To the Caribbean . . . Hawaii . . . Tours of Canada . . . Tours of the U.S.A.

As she grew older, conscious of the strain of continually travelling alone, she would sometimes ask a friend to accompany her. Travelling with Joy opened up new vistas of faith to them. On the one hand Joy's natural lack of organisation in all matters apart from the work of Gospel Recordings often landed her in awkward situations that could have been avoided by care or forethought. On the other hand her confident faith that the Lord would work things out for her in spite of everything proved well-founded.

'It is an experience of watching miracles performed to travel with her,' wrote one of her travelling companions. 'The Lord answers prayer for her in such a way that one woman commented, "He doesn't answer prayer for me like that." Of course, I believe the secret is not only her faith but the fact she is so in fellowship that she asks what He delights in answering.'

When she was 71 she set off on another trip around the world, with an air ticket to take her to 35 countries. She lost the ticket, along with her passport and health card, when travelling on a bus in Nairobi. She and her companion had agreed it would save money to go that way rather than take a taxi from the Mission Guest House where they were staying, and Joy's handbag was rifled on the crowded vehicle. She did not discover anything was missing, however, until the next day, when they were on their way to get their visas for India.

No passport. No air ticket. No health card.

'Rejoice!' said Joy. 'Rejoice. There must be a reason. This is good rejoicing practice.' Her travelling companion did not immediately view it in that light, but when in less than twenty-four hours Joy was provided with a new passport, new health card and new air ticket, she gasped. 'It was simply amazing, for the airline had to telex to Los Angeles for permission to rewrite the ticket and they had to telex back all those places and routes – the ticket was about an inch thick! Then she had to get some more injections, but it was a miracle how quickly these were secured.'

On another occasion they arrived at a tiny airport in the Sudan where there was no telephone, no telephone book, and where nobody seemed to know anything about the Sudan Interior Mission. Joy had hoped to meet the missionaries there to discuss records distribution and the possibility of doing further recording. Her custom was to arrive unannounced, then phone someone she knew or had heard about and enquire about accommodation, a habit which some of her travelling companions found rather disconcerting. They couldn't help wondering if the arrival of two unexpected visitors would be as welcome and as convenient as Joy took for granted. She herself was always cheerfully willing to move out of her own room at Witmer Street if an extra bed were needed, and it did not occur to her that other hostesses might be less adaptable. On this occasion, since she had not made a note of the S.I.M. address, there seemed nothing else for it but to take the next plane out. An hour before it was due to leave, however, Joy was chatting to an old lady at the airport, and discovered that her nephew, who had come to see her off, worked for the S.I.M. . . .

They didn't take the next plane out after all.

The culminating excitement of that particular incident was to be taken to a Sunday service where some of the congregation were second generation Christians, children of those who had come to know the Lord through Gospel Recordings records.

They went to some thirty countries and forty-odd cities, and only about six times were they met at the airport. In most cases no-one knew they were coming. Yet it seemed that there was always someone who could direct them to the places Joy wanted to go to, or the people she wanted to meet.

Her travelling companions noticed other things, too. Joy suffered from arthritis and was often in pain, but she never complained – only rejoiced. 'And her singleness of purpose was something to behold. She had but one thought in mind, and that was Gospel Recordings.'

Her activity and her influence extended beyond her organisation, however. She had travelled so widely, addressed so many meetings in all sorts of places, that everywhere she went were people who knew her or knew about her. When they were in Singapore Joy was invited to speak at a conference, and at the close of her address one of the young preachers present told the others that he was in the ministry because he had heard Joy speak in his seminary. In Perth, Australia, the same thing happened. She was invited to speak in a church where the minister announced it was through hearing her, years ago, that he was a minister today.

She had been invited to attend the World Congress on Evangelisation in Lausanne, sponsored by Billy Graham, as one of the comparatively few women delegates, and here again, she was constantly being greeted by people who knew her. One man, over six feet tall, engaged in Christian radio broadcasting, had used some of the records, and chuckled when he saw her. 'Here we big people sit at home,' he said, 'and little Joy goes out into the bush country and does the work!'

Joy described the whole Lausanne experience as being like a foretaste of heaven, a preview of the time when those from every tribe and nation will come to worship Christ. Yet it was shot through with sobering reminders that that time had not yet come. 'Much of the suffering of people around the world was portrayed to us,' she wrote. 'The huge population clock in the dining hall reminded us how many thousands were being born each day of the conference. It was fantastic to see how the need of the world to hear the good news of Jesus is ever increasing. The need for our recordings was newly impressed upon my heart.'

She arrived back from the seven months' tour that had taken her round the world in time to attend the Board Meetings of Gospel Recordings in Los Angeles, where Robert Thompson, having made a worldwide survey of missionary work, gave a masterly summary of the situation as he saw it. The urgency of the hour that had been impressed upon her had been even more deeply impressed upon him. He saw, as well as she, the strategic part that Gospel Recordings could play in those areas where time seemed to be running out, where the opportunities for evangelism might not last much longer.

'Look at Vietnam, for instance . . .' Something must be done and done quickly.

It was agreed that a conference should be called of the leaders of the G.R. centres worldwide to co-ordinate the work, unite resources and press forward, especially to those isolated tribes, the by-passed, the resistant, those who had never heard the Gospel in their own tongue. The conference was called for June of that year, for there was no time to lose.

There was another reason for calling such a conference. Joy was in her seventies now, and the question arose, 'How much longer can she continue? Whatever happens, the work must go on.' At that memorable conference, not only was the aim of reaching every last little tribe on earth with the Gospel re-affirmed, but the Gospel Recordings International Council was established.

*   *   *

One day, on returning to Los Angeles from one of her speaking tours, Joy was told of a visitor who had come to look round Gospel Recordings. Many visitors came for that purpose, but this one was unusual because of something he told the staff member who showed him around. The elderly widower, recently re-married, said in the course of conversation, 'I knew Joy Ridderhof when we were both young. As a matter of fact, I asked her to marry me — but she turned me down.'

Joy had no need to enquire his name. She knew he was

Francis. She looked back to the occasion, forty years ago, when he had spoken of marriage and she hadn't known whether he was proposing or not, and had reacted in a way that he had evidently taken as being a refusal. It was the only time in her life when she had been seriously prepared to marry anyone, and she remembered the bewilderment, the grief of that weekend when she hoped he would broach the subject again, and when he had walked off with another girl instead. She understood now. He had acted that way because he was hurt, not because he did not care.

She understood something else, too. She understood why it had happened, why what she had so deeply desired at the time had not been granted to her. And now she thought of the little discs whirling in so many countries, so many remote regions, proclaiming with voices the listeners could understand that Jesus gives life, life that endures . . . Oh the joy, the joy of that! Not for anything would she wish to exchange such joy now. How absolutely right it had been to rejoice, even out of the pain then!

12

As at the Beginning

'Say, Ann, have you seen this?' asked Joy, holding up a book she had been looking through. 'They call it a handbook, but it looks like a pretty thick volume to me. Handbook of instructions. Everything a recordist needs to know. And it's *ours!* It's a Gospel Recordings publication, compiled by our staff. Larry was showing it yesterday, at the seminar, to that group of young people taking the training course. I hadn't seen it before.'

Ann knew of it. She was glad that the small handbook she had written years before was being replaced by a more complete and up to date book of instructions. She glanced through it appreciatively.

'We could have done with it ourselves when we started, couldn't we?' she said with a chuckle. Then she went on more thoughtfully, 'It's been coming to me recently, how we had to feel our way, and figure out a technique for recording using an interpreter. We found it out in a very rough way. And now these techniques have been perfected and refined till we have a whole handbook of instructions, run seminars to train recordists, not only here but in Canada, India, Australia...!' The training seminars were the outcome of the international conference that had been held in June, 1975, when the challenge of the peoples still unreached had been faced anew, and it had affirmed that

Gospel Recordings is a partnership of organisations which

*exists to communicate the Gospel of the Lord Jesus Christ
to all people in their own language.*

and that

*The first priority is to record the Gospel in the unrecorded
languages by 1981.*

The quickest way to achieve the primary object so that
every tiny tribe on earth would have a chance to hear the
Gospel in its own tongue was to teach the unique techniques of
interpreter-recording to people on the spot. Perhaps the most
strategically placed of all the seminars was the one conducted
in India by Enoch Anthony, himself an Indian. The 1975
survey had revealed that there were more unreached tribes in
Asia than in Africa and South America put together – and
that a large proportion of them were in India. And now, for the
first time, it was Indian, not western field recordists who were
preparing to strike the trail for the tribes in Gujarat,
Rajasthan, Maharashtra. Well, at least they would have a
handbook to refer to!

Joy and Ann looked at each other, and smiled. Ann had
recently returned to Los Angeles for a holiday after being
away for several years. Her recording trips had taken her
through Europe, South Africa, the Near East, and to remote
places in Central Asia about which she said very little but
where she had captured languages most people had never
heard of. Sitting there now in Joy's attic room where it had all
started, conscious that others were carrying on what they had
begun, the two friends, were in the mood for reminiscing.

'It didn't look like very much could come out of what we
were doing in those early days, did it?' said Ann. There had
never been a time when she had doubted, but even she had not
foreseen how much would come of their efforts. 'Think of
that trip to Mexico! Remember how hard it was lugging that
90lb recorder in and out of the car, using those glass-based
blanks to cut the records?'

'Yes, I remember! Going with it to colleges and places here

in the States, too.' Joy screwed up her forehead, trying to remember something. 'I don't know if anybody ever helped us to carry that thing?'

'I know we did it enough times ourselves to feel no-one ever did!' said Ann. 'Then remember when we went to the Philippines and had to use a generator to make the electricity?'

'I'll never forget that!' replied Joy feelingly. 'I'll never forget that hot, hot climate and cranking that generator. Blah-blah-blah then stop. Blah-blah-blah then stop. There was I right in the middle of the street with it, as far away as I could get from you so that the noise wouldn't come over on the recording. Crank, crank, crank, blah-blah-blah . . . ! That was terrific. And then we had to get it back into the car! Whew! The heat! By the way, how did we ever think we could do anything without a car?'

'It just shows how little we knew,' laughed Ann. 'Coming across the Pacific with all those hundreds of kilos of baggage, preparing to travel widely, and no car! But the Lord knows these things ahead of time, and He has everything worked out. Think of the way that missionary lent us his car!'

'And the way Al and Herman made that little battery-run recorder, and got it to us just at the right time!' They had had many such experiences through the years since then, but the trip to the Philippines always stood out exceptionally vividly. They had been so deeply convinced that God had sent them there. Even when circumstances were the most discouraging they had stuck to it that He would not let them down, nor allow their work to be in vain.

'That's why I still get excited when I read letters like this one that I read the other day,' she said. 'It's from a Filipino who was working near an area noted for criminals, and he was very reluctant to go there. 'I am not very much of a coward but I would like to live yet at this time,' he wrote. But when the gramophone and the records arrived, he decided he would try. 'I thought they might be allured to listen and just be willing to listen to God's Word. And God worked it that way. The message pierced their hearts and now even alone I can go to those places. We have already more than 100 sympathisers. I call them sympathisers because they are still very young, even though they have accepted Christ.'

'Oh, that's wonderful. I've never heard that one before.' Joy was always moved by such reports. One of the regular tasks in the G.R. offices was to collect excerpts from letters telling of results from the records, and Joy was never tired of reading them. They were tangible evidence that the seeds being sown were bearing fruit. All the patient and often hazardous work of the recordists, all the painstaking labour in the Los Angeles studios on the tapes that were received, then the steady processes through which the captured voice passed in the factory until it was eventually pressed into records, then all the careful packing and dispatching was in vain unless that captured voice was heard at last by those who could understand it. The task of distribution in the countries for which the records were intended was one that often demanded as much attention as the initial obtaining of the records. To encourage and expedite distribution had been one of Joy's main objects in the many journeys she had taken. She was only really satisfied when she knew that they had reached their destinations, and accomplished their original purpose.

'Do you remember when we were in the Philippines we thought we had gone to the very end of the globe?' Joy continued. 'You've been so many trips to so many places since then, Ann, that I couldn't keep track of them.' A practical question came to mind, one that could be put between friends. 'How have you managed about money?'

'Oh, we carry on the same as we always have,' replied Ann. 'If the Lord tells Marlene and me to go somewhere we just look to Him to send in the needed funds, and He does it. We never have it all before we start. I don't suppose we ever shall. He sends money to us from all sorts of unexpected places and at unexpected times. But you know all about that.'

Yes, Joy knew all about that.

'You know, Ann,' she said, as a memory rose up in her mind. 'When I talked to you about going to Nigeria ... After we'd done that world trip, you and Sanna and I together, and when we got back here I just knew there was so much of Africa we hadn't touched. And I talked to you about going to Nigeria. Oh, I just hated to think of you going over there alone.'

'Yes, I hated it too,' said Ann quietly. It had been one of the greatest tests of her life, to face up to going to Africa alone. She had been prepared to follow Joy to the ends of the earth, for Joy was a leader and Ann, by nature, was a follower. But to go without Joy, to take the responsibility, make the arrangements, lead the way . . . To be asked to go alone!

'But you went!' said Joy. 'You went! You said, "Joy, you will pray for me, won't you?" and I said, "Why, Ann, of course I'll pray for you!" and you went!'

Joy's memory was in full flight now, speeding back over the years. Whoever had come and gone in Gospel Recordings, Ann had always been there, steadily plodding on with her tape recorder, capturing languages. Always to be relied on, always ready to respond when she was convinced God's call lay behind a new challenge.

'Europe, too!' continued Joy. 'I was thinking so much about Europe. You'd been in Africa for some years, and you were back with us again, and I just felt in my heart that we must do something about Europe. I knew that there were so many areas of Europe just as badly off as any country in the world, one way or another. But I couldn't go, just like I couldn't go to Nigeria when I asked you to go there. I was going to have to ask you to go out alone.

'I hated to, Ann. I really did, because to go to Europe I knew wouldn't be easy for me and I knew it wouldn't be any easier for you. But I just felt we must. So I asked you if you would go to Europe. And you said, "But Joy, I don't know any of the languages of Europe. I don't know French. I don't know German. What would I do in Europe?" '

Ann smiled and nodded. It was easy to look back now and smile, though it had not been so easy to look forward into the unknown, to contemplate stepping out alone into the confusing jangle of sophisticated, go-ahead nations of western Europe.

She remembered arriving in England after the usual correspondence, to get the advice of the Gospel Recordings Board and
staff there as to the best way to do recording work in Europe.

'They don't speak much English over there,' they had said
to her, rather dubiously. 'You really need to speak French and
German at least, as well as English, to get around in Europe
...' Then they had added, 'But there's a girl here who's just
come into our work, and she speaks and writes both. Marlene
Muhr — she's French, heard Joy speak when she was at
Swansea Bible College, and felt called to Gospel Recordings
...'

'So there you were!' said Joy triumphantly. 'That's the way
God works. For twelve years you two have worked together in
Europe, and other places, too. Oh, praise God for the way He
does answer our prayers. When He sends us out He knows
what we need and whom we need, and He supplies.'

He had supplied in the past, and He was still supplying, in
ways they could not fathom. Gospel Recordings had entered a
new era. No longer could it be labelled, rather sweepingly, as
being a missionary organisation run by a woman. Joy was still
Director, but shared her position now with a man, and one in
the prime of life. John Gray had been appointed Associate
Director in 1976, and was already shouldering the administrative responsibilities.

He hadn't seen how he could accept the position when he
was first approached. There was no-one to take his place as
Canadian Director, and he was warned that it might take a
very long time to obtain permission to enter the U.S.A. and
settle there. But when Edwin Tomlinson, whose years with the
Sudan Interior Mission in Ethiopia had been followed by a
long period in administration at home, expressed his conviction that the Lord was calling him into G.R., and when
permission was obtained from the U.S. Government eleven
days after application for John and Lillian Gray to live in the
States for a year, he didn't see how he could refuse. The timing
of events was just as significant as had been the arrival in India
of Joy to say categorically that Bangalore was the place where
G.R. should establish its factory, when he was wondering what

to do with the land around the Ebenezer Church right there in Bangalore. He had to say 'Yes'!

So Joy was no longer bearing the burden of leadership alone, and with the reorganisation that had taken place since the 1975 Conference the future was looking brighter than for several years. She was full of enthusiasm.

'Now we've made a goal,' she said, referring to the aim of getting all known languages by 1981. 'It's laughable to most people. It's ridiculous to some. It's wrong to others. Making a goal like that when this country is closed, that country is closed, something else is closed! That's what people say.

'But Christ said the Gospel was to be preached to every creature, and He wouldn't have said it if it wasn't possible! I believe that the most difficult place on earth can open at the time we need to go in. But why is He going to open a place when we don't go into the places already open? Why should He open a closed door when we haven't gone through those that are open?'

'Well, Joy, I'm right with you,' said Ann. 'I guess what we need to do is to pray "Lord, increase our faith." ' She left soon after that. Her furlough was nearly over and she was preparing to return to Europe. A strenuous programme lay before her, and one never knew what unexpected opportunities might be ripening!

Joy sank back in her chair, feeling rather exhausted. She didn't know why she'd been getting so tired lately. The doctor hadn't been able to discover the cause, either. Maybe those tests she'd been having at the clinic would reveal something. There was so much to be done, all those meetings ahead that she was booked to speak at, she simply must go to them. Well, she'd been played out, prostrated many times before, and in pain, too, but the Lord had raised her up, given her strength, and everything had proved to have been for the best. It always would!

Meanwhile, it was time for her thanksgivings for the day, before going to bed. So many things to say 'Thank you' for! She liked to keep them all on record, so she switched on her little cassette.

I'm thankful that I have this lovely suite here for my rooms, and the open porch in the hot weather.

Thank you, Lord, for helping me to get those difficult letters written.

I'm so glad there's a little breeze coming up now.

Thank you, Lord, for all the good things to eat this noon. Peas, carrots and corn and I don't know what else. So delicious. All mixed together. Such a good meal. And it was so nice having that get-together in the house . . . and the ice cream.

Thank you for those helpers that are coming to help the work in England. It's real good! Bless them, Lord.

Thank you for the dictating that I got done today . . .

And for the Grays. Bless them tonight. Bless them in a special way. Undertake for them, be near to them, uplift them, glorify Thyself in them.

I'm so glad someone fixed Marie's toaster. It makes it so much easier for her. And for her helping me and working on my clothes. I do appreciate that.

I'm so glad I made the ice tea with some ice and some lemon in it. And so glad that I had those real beautiful lemons from our own trees.

Thank you for Ann, Lord. All that she's done all these years — such a good pal. Bless her, Lord.

For that man who's going to Bangladesh to try to open the way for those records to be sent in there. Help him Lord, help him to call upon Thee . . .

Lord, please show me the solution to this watch that's gone wrong.

Lord, bless the records, wherever they're being played all over the world. Oh, Lord, how wonderful, how wonderful Thou art! I praise Thee, I praise Thee, I praise Thee. Thank you, Lord. Thank you for everything . . .

I'll go to sleep now . . .

Goodnight, Lord . . .

EPILOGUE

On Wednesday, December 19, 1984 Joy quietly left behind her "earthen vessel" to enter into the presence of her beloved Lord. She was just over 81 years old. Her successor as General Director, Larry Allmon, speaking at the private funeral service, said he felt the verse that seemed to fit Joy's life best was II Corinthians 4:7 ". . . we have this treasure in earthen vessels to show that the transcendent power belongs to God and not to us." Joy knew and accepted that principle long ago, he said, and it had freed her to be available, and useable, and expendable — always with great rejoicing.

It had freed her to relinquish responsibility when the time came, too, which is sometimes the most difficult thing of all to do. Larry had accepted the leadership of Gospel Recordings in 1978 at the request of the U.S. Board of Directors, and the transition was easy for Joy, who truly welcomed it. From that time on, Joy became known officially as the "Founder" while Larry served as General Director.

Yet for him that appointment had come about suddenly and unexpectedly. He had not even been a staff member, merely the newest Board Member when he was asked to represent them at the international meeting of the six autonomous Gospel Recordings organizations to be held in Bangalore, India, in January of that year. The five former "branches" were now fully autonomous centres — each with its own organizational structure, policies, and priorities. Representatives were coming from Sydney, Australia; Gloucester, Great Britain; Bangalore, India; Toronto, Canada; and Cape Town, South Africa. John and Lillian

Gray would be there, too, on their way to Hong Kong to oversea the manufacture of the revolutionary handcranked GRIP cassette player which had been developed by the Gospel Recordings - Australia organization. But it was as the plane flew quietly some 40,000 feet above the Pacific Ocean that Larry Allmon was suddenly impressed with a deep, unshakeable conviction that God's plan for him and his family was taking a new, dramatic turn. By the time he reached India he knew what God was calling him to do. He was to make application to join Gospel Recordings as a full-time staff member!

It came as rather a shock, for he was fully engaged as Personnel Director for a large public school district in San Diego County at the time. Before that his main job had been Bible teaching — first in Morocco with the "Voice of Tangier;" then in Madrid, Spain, with The Evangelical Alliance Mission; then he had pastored two churches in California and been involved in teaching and administration in a Christian high school. With that background he wondered what he could do at Gospel Recordings since he was not technically oriented or young enough to be a field recordist.

The U.S.A. Board of Directors and staff at Los Angeles did not wonder. At that June Board meeting in 1978, Larry and his wife were accepted as staff members, and he was asked to assume responsibilities as the next General Director.

Joy was still occupying her tiny flat on the Gospel Recordings compound. Her physical condition was deteriorating and her memory failing, but she was always ready to pray and to rejoice, as everyone who visited her knew. Then, after her birthday in March, 1984, she had to go into the hospital for surgery; and although the operation was successful, it had become apparent that it would no longer be possible for any one person to be responsible to give her the care she needed.

But God was preparing out of His abundant provision for His servant. Just when it became necessary to relocate her, a vacancy occurred in the Health Care Unit at "Quaker Gardens" in Stanton, California, where she had a number of friends.

During those last months it was very difficult for Joy to communicate (her speech was not usually intelligible), except in prayer. Her sweet spirit, however, still blessed those who came in daily contact with her, as well as the visitors who came to see her. Though she was past being able to remember all that the Lord had done through her life, the work which she began out of faithful obedience to God was continuing all around the world.

At the large memorial service held on Sunday, January 13, 1985 there were many present from Joy's past: her sister, Amy Hillis; Ann Sherwood and Sanna Barlow Rossi; Stuart and Molly Mill from Australia; Robertson McQuilkin, President of Columbia Bible College; Bob Bowman of the Far East Broadcasting Company; besides Virginia Miller, Herman Dyk, and many others whose lives had been permanently changed by Joy's ministry during her earthly sojourn. One could only imagine what it was like for her, who had joined the multitudes of redeemed people in heavenly worship of the King of Kings — many who had first heard the Gospel message on those little records and cassettes!

She has passed out of our sight now, but her works follow her.

At the original headquarters of the work she founded in Los Angeles, the Mission was re-examining its principles, which were subsequently identified as the following:

"To Every One In His Own Tongue" — that is, that every unreached people group (and by extension, every individual) should have the opportunity to hear the recorded Gospel message in its own language or dialect.

"Freely Ye Have Received . . . Freely Give" — this practice would be maintained in order to reflect the very nature of the Gospel itself. No charge would be made for the priceless, message-bearing recordings and players.

"In Everything, By Prayer" — a renewed determination to make the work move ahead by prayer, continuing

to spend at least one day each week in praising
God and intercession.

"Pray the Lord of the Harvest for Laborers" — just as
the first workers were brought by the Lord to the
work in answer to prayer, so the Mission would
continue to "recruit" additional staff members by
praying them in.

"Rejoice, Give Thanks, and Sing!" — the discipline
Joy adopted in making it a deliberate choice to rejoice, especially when there was no visible cause for
such rejoicing, would be encouraged both within
the staff and among the friends of the Mission.

"Make Known His Deeds Among the People" — the
original "two-fold purpose" of the work included
this passion for encouraging believers in the churches
by sharing with them reports of the constant stream
of miracles experienced in this part of the Lord's
harvest.

"God Shall Supply All Our Needs — By Faith" —
there was to be no equivocating on this basic means
for financing the work: just a simple trust in God to
move the hearts of individual believers within His
Body without any public mention of financial needs
or asking for donations directly or indirectly.

In 1986 there were eleven nationalities (American,
Brazilian, British, Colombian, Dutch, French, German,
Nepalese, Nigerian, Singaporean, and a former South
African) represented on the staff at Gospel Recordings -
U.S.A. working in Africa, Europe, North and South
America and Asia. All had come to the Mission with the
same conviction that God had led them to the work, and
all had come fully trusting in the Lord's ability to provide
all their needs from day to day. And the miracles go
on . . .

Typical of the way the Lord still provides for the work,

was the recent account of just one week in Los Angeles. Financially, the work had nearly come to a stand-still. On that Monday morning the General Fund balance was $413.10. This was *all* the money in hand to pay current bills (amounting to $3,826.63) due to be paid by Friday!

The mail for Monday and Tuesday brought in additional gifts totalling $779.20. That meant there was only $1,192.30 towards the payment of financial obligations which included rents, some overseas base expenses, telephone bills and several other items. To make matters worse, insurance policies were threatened with cancellation as there was not enough on hand to pay the annual premiums. Nor was there any money in the postage meter that week for mailing out those precious packages of Gospel records and cassettes and players (about $1,200 was needed.)

Consistent with the Mission's experience in trusting the Lord day by day, there were no "reserve funds" — only the reassuring awareness that the principal Resource was and is, in fact, God Himself.

The total need? Close to $12,000! On hand? $1,192 in the General Fund, and $3,306 in the insurance premium fund — *PLUS* the promise of God to supply *all* the needs of those who trust in Him!

On that Wednesday Prayer Day, the Staff divided into seven small bands, moving periodically to seven different locations around the office and factory where each group was led in a review of each of the basic principles of the Mission. The promises of the Word of God became so fresh and encouraging to the group as they again made it their choice to rejoice, especially difficult in the light of the bleak financial situation.

While opening the morning's mail on Thursday, Marjorie Johnson startled nearby co-workers with a series of loud "hoorays." The reason? A check representing the proceeds from a Living Trust amounting to $9,224.39! God's precise timing was a source of renewed awe at His working, for the donor had passed away in 1981 — *four and one half years previously!* Yet on the very day following another deep testing of rejoicing faith, the Lord brought in the prayed-for finances! There could be absolutely no mistaking *His* hand in providing the needed funds on that day!

No appeal for funds had been made (Gospel Recordings - U.S.A.'s 47-year-old commitment!);

No manipulating of bank accounts and balances (there were none to manipulate!);

No mentioning of financial needs to potential donors, not even by hinting!

All together, gifts received on Thursday and Friday came to $10,405.39!

All bills were paid—all needs were met by God! Again!

Here was a fresh, new instance of the faithfulness of the Lord so similar to those experienced many times since the beginning of the work of Gospel Recordings.

And the latest count of languages and dialects in which the life-changing Gospel message has been recorded? **4,377!**

"TO GOD BE THE GLORY, GREAT THINGS HE HATH DONE!"